The Essential Guide to
Group Communication

The Essential Guide to Group Communication

Dan O'Hair
University of Oklahoma

Mary O. Wiemann
Santa Barbara City College

BEDFORD / ST. MARTIN'S

Boston ♦ New York

Manufactured in the United States of America.

9 8 7 6 5
o n m

For information, write: Bedford/St. Martin's, 75 Arlington Street, Boston, MA 02116   (617-399-4000)

ISBN-10: 0-312-45194-6
ISBN-13: 978-0-312-45194-3

PREFACE

The Essential Guide to Group Communication is a versatile supplement for students who need a brief, topical introduction to key concepts in group communication. It has been designed as a flexible option for use in a variety of speech courses, including introduction to communication classes that do not use a traditional full-size text, "public speaking plus" classes that concentrate on public speaking but also include units on group communication along with other communication topics, and any class where instructors want to give students a brief but thorough introduction to group communication. Developed primarily for use with O'Hair, Stewart, and Rubenstein's *A Speaker's Guidebook* and *A Pocket Guide to Public Speaking,* it can be used as well with a wide variety of communication texts.

The Essential Guide to Group Communication helps students identify and understand core issues in group communication quickly and effectively through an approach that combines a solid foundation in communication theory with a clear emphasis on student skill acquisition. Topic coverage includes:

- An overview of communication theory (Chapter 1)

- Discussions of the definition of group communication, the benefits of group communication, and the ways group communication differs from other forms of communication (Chapter 1)

- Participation in group communication: characteristics of effective groups and group members, techniques for improving group communication, special types of groups, and evaluating group communication competence (Chapter 2)

- Leadership and decision making: the roles of leadership, factors influencing decision making, the process of decision making, and evaluating decision making (Chapter 3)

- Organizational communication: the need for effective communication in organizations, how organizational communication differs from other types of communication, and developing effective group communication skills (Chapter 4)

FEATURES

The approach and content of this text are based on the extensive experience of Dan O'Hair and Mary Wiemann teaching group communication in the classroom, and the pedagogy is based on the successful innovations developed in *A Speaker's Guidebook.*

Throughout *The Essential Guide,* you will find useful *checklists,* offering step-by-step directions, assessment checks, and content review checks. Widely praised by reviewers for their precision and conciseness, these checklists help students understand key concepts and assess their own learning.

Compelling features throughout the text highlight issues vital to group communicators. *Group Communication in Cultural Perspective* boxes help students understand the cultural requirements of group speech situations. They feature topics such as cross-cultural views of group norms and diversity in the workforce. *Ethically Speaking* boxes emphasize the importance of ethics in group communication situations and include such topics as responsibility in the transactional communication process and balancing personal and group goals.

This booklet is available either as a stand-alone text; or packaged with *A Speaker's Guidebook, A Pocket Guide to Public Speaking,* and a number of other Bedford/St. Martin's communication titles including the booklet *The Essential Guide to Interpersonal Communication.* Please note that because the booklets have been designed to stand alone, the coverage of communication theory in both *The Essential Guide to Interpersonal Communication* and *The Essential Guide to Group Communication* is identical. For information on these or other Bedford/St. Martin's Communication texts, or to contact your local sales representative, please visit our Web site at <**bedfordstmartins.com**>.

CONTENTS

Preface   v

1 Foundations of Communicating in Small Groups and Teams   1

What Is Communication?   1
Communication Is Symbolic   1
Communication Is a Shared Code   2
Communication Is Linked to Culture   3
    BOX: Group Communication in Cultural Perspective: Comparing
    Communication Norms   4
Communication Is Intentional   4
Communication Is Mediated   5
Communication Is Transactional   6

What Is Group Communication?   6
    BOX: Ethically Speaking: Your Ethical Responsibility in the
    Transactional Communication Process   6

What Are the Benefits of Effective Group Communication?   7

How Does Group Communication Differ from Other Forms of
Communication?   7
Group Communication Means More Interactants   8
Group Communication Means More Complex Relationships   8

2 Participating in Small Group Communication   10

What Makes a Good Group Member?   10
Applying Critical Thinking in Groups   10
Making Use of Attributions in Groups   12
Monitoring Perceptions in Groups   13
Overcoming Communication Apprehension in Groups   13
    ✓ CHECKLIST: How Well Do You Interact in a Group Setting?   15

What Makes a Good Group?   16
Interdependence in Groups   16
Cohesion in Groups   17
Recognizing and Avoiding Groupthink in Groups   18
Applying Productive Conflict in Groups   18
Establishing Norms in Groups   19

The Group Image in Groups   *20*
   BOX: Group Communication in Cultural Perspective: Cross-Cultural
   View of Group Norms   20

Techniques for Improving Communication in Groups   21
   Goal Setting in Groups   *21*
     ✓ CHECKLIST: A Group Leader's Strategies for Effective
     Goal Setting   22
   Agenda Setting in Groups   *23*
     BOX: Ethically Speaking: Balancing Group Goals with
     Personal Goals   23
   Deliberation and Participation in Groups   *24*
   Roles in Groups   *25*
     ✓ CHECKLIST: Strategies for Encouraging Group Participation   25
   Networks in Groups   *27*

Special Group Types and Techniques   29
   The Nominal Group Technique   *29*
   Self-Managing Teams   *30*

Evaluating Competence in Group Communication   31

3   *Leadership and Decision Making in Groups and Teams*   **32**

The Role of Leadership in Group Communication   32
   What Is Leadership?   *32*
   Types of Leadership   *33*
     ✓ CHECKLIST: Characteristics of Authoritarian Leaders   33
     ✓ CHECKLIST: Characteristics of Participative Leaders   34
   Shared Leadership   *35*
   Effective Leadership   *36*
     BOX: Group Communication in Cultural Perspective:
     Culture and Shared Leadership   36

Factors Influencing Decision Making in Groups and Teams   37
   Understanding the Variables Affecting Group Decision Making   *37*
     BOX: Ethically Speaking: Ethics and O-Rings   39
   Developing Group Decision-Making Skills   *40*
   Clarifying Group Values and Goals   *41*
     ✓ CHECKLIST: Values Clarification   42
   Managing Group Expectations   *43*
   Dealing with Time Pressures in Groups   *44*
   Working Through Conflict   *45*

The Process of Decision Making in Groups and Teams   46
   Identify the Problem   *46*
   Conduct Research   *47*
   Establish Guidelines and Criteria   *48*
   Generate Alternatives   *48*
   Evaluate Alternatives   *49*

Select the Best Alternative   49
Implement the Solution   50
Evaluate the Results   50
Evaluating the Decision-Making Competence of Groups and Teams   51
Group Evaluations   51
Individual Evaluations   53

4 *Communicating in Organizations*   54

The Need for Effective Communication in Organizations   54
How Does Organizational Communication Differ from Other Types of
Communication?   54
    BOX: Group Communication in Cultural Perspective: Cultural
    Diversity in the Workforce   55
Organizational Culture   55
Organizational Systems   56
Organizational Relationships   59
    ✓ CHECKLIST: Strategies for Superiors and Subordinates   60
Developing Effective Skills in Organizational Communication   61
Use Communication Channels   62
Use Communication Networks   63
Negotiate Effectively   65
    ✓ CHECKLIST: Strategies for Effective Negotiation   66
Practice Mentoring   66
    ✓ CHECKLIST: Finding a Mentor   67
Respond to Sexual Harassment   68
    BOX: Ethically Speaking: Ethics and Sexual Harassment   68
Master Communication Technology   69
    ✓ CHECKLIST: Strategies for Addressing Sexual Harassment   69
    ✓ CHECKLIST: Tips for Communicating via Telephone   70
    ✓ CHECKLIST: Tips for Effective Teleconferences   71
    ✓ CHECKLIST: E-mail Etiquette   72
Summary   73
Glossary   74
Notes   78

Foundations of Communicating in Small Groups and Teams **1**

Remember the adage "two heads are better than one"? We know that when two people come together to solve a problem, their combined creativity, knowledge, and experience usually make it easier for a particular task to be accomplished. Well, if "two heads are better than one," then three or more should have even greater potential. To achieve this potential, however, it is important to first understand what *communication* and *group communication* are, and then to understand the factors involved in small group communication. Through this understanding, we can develop the skills necessary to be competent group members—in both formal and informal groups.

We all participate in communication with groups of people; sometimes that communication is successful, and sometimes it is not. Often, our success or failure depends on how well we understand the dynamics of communication in small groups. As we become aware of the factors that influence relationships, we are better able to develop, maintain, or terminate relationships in our own lives. In addition, we are able to develop the social skills needed in formal as well as informal contexts.

Groups are everywhere. You are part of many groups now, and your involvement in groups is likely to increase in the future. Yet, being part of these groups and working well in them are two different matters. Learning more about what groups are, how they work, and how to work within them will help you become an effective and competent communicator in groups.

WHAT IS COMMUNICATION?

The better you understand the process of communication, the more likely you will be to use your communication skills appropriately and effectively—and the more likely you will be to create satisfying, productive, and meaningful group interactions in your life. In order to improve your own knowledge and understanding of group communication, you first need to understand the basic communication process.

Communication is a process that is defined by six characteristics:

- Communication is **symbolic**.
- Communication is a **shared code**.
- Communication is linked to **culture**.

- Communication is **intentional**.
- Communication is **mediated**.
- Communication is **transactional**.

Behavior that clearly possesses all of these characteristics (to one degree or another) is *communication* and can be analyzed as such. Keep in mind, however, that the line between what is communication and what is not can sometimes be blurry. Some messages are more obviously communicative than others. For example, when six-year-old Ellie sticks her tongue out at Jake, that's communication that is very purposeful; but when twenty-one-year-old Sara makes one-second eye contact with Alan across the room, her intention to communicate is less clear.

It is useful, therefore, for us to be able to analyze messages in terms of these characteristics, so that we can understand why communication problems occur and how we might solve them. Using this approach will help you to evaluate the various messages you receive on a daily basis. Let's take a look at each of these six characteristics in detail.

COMMUNICATION IS SYMBOLIC

Behavior is symbolic when it has an arbitrary relationship to an object. **Symbols** are arbitrary constructions that are related to the objects to which they refer. The stronger the connection between symbol and object, the clearer the intended meaning.

The most **symbolic behavior** is language. Every language is a code that allows those who know it to transform speech into meaningful messages. There is no particular reason why the arbitrary transcription of the letters T-R-E-E should represent a very large variety of plant form. But in our code, American English, it does.

Although spoken language is the primary form of symbolic behavior in our culture, nonverbal behavior can also be symbolic. Hand gestures, in particular, may have symbolic properties. For example, joining the thumb and forefinger in a circle while extending the other three fingers means "okay" in middle-class U.S. culture. Gestures of this sort, "autonomous gestures,"[1] operate in much the same way as language. That is to say, we do not need words to know what they mean.

COMMUNICATION IS A SHARED CODE

In order for communication to take place, the participants must share the **code** (the set of symbol-meaning relationships) used to **encode** and **decode** messages.

Speaking a common language is the most obvious example of sharing a communication code. Keep in mind, however, that although we tend to assume that because people share a language code they share common meanings for the symbols they use, this is clearly not the case. For example, American travelers to and from England are frequently surprised (and amused) that the same words refer to different things in the two versions of the English language. A British person in a U.S. drugstore asking for a rubber would be sent to the pharmaceutical counter for a condom rather than to the stationery aisle for an eraser.

Keep in mind, however, that a symbol can take on new meaning if at least two people agree that it will have that meaning for them. Social groups use this technique to establish their uniqueness and to create boundaries between themselves and the "outside" world.

Speaking a common language is the most obvious example of sharing a communication code, but it is not the only one. Each culture also shares specific meanings for gestures, tones of voice, and facial expressions. Some aspects of these codes cross cultural boundaries, making them especially powerful communication vehicles. Facial expressions of surprise, fear, disgust, anger, happiness, and sadness seem to have universal meanings.[2] Thus, they allow people from different cultures to understand each other's most basic feelings, even when they cannot speak the same language.

COMMUNICATION IS LINKED TO CULTURE

If you've ever traveled to a different country or even through the different neighborhoods of a city, you know that communication is difficult to separate from culture. We use the term **culture** to refer to the shared beliefs, values, and practices of a group of people. A group's culture includes the language or languages used by group members as well as the norms and rules about how behavior can appropriately be displayed and how it should be understood.

The most obvious connection between communication and culture is language. People from different cultures usually speak different languages, which are often unintelligible to "strangers." But the communication-culture relationship goes well beyond obvious language differences. Cultural experience and everyday life strongly influence how language influences our interpretation of the world around us.[3] For example, an interior decorator may find it useful, or even necessary, to distinguish among lavender, mauve, burgundy, violet, plum, lilac, magenta, amethyst, and heliotrope. For many of us, however, these fine distinctions are unimportant; purple is purple!

Our nonverbal behavior also is wrapped up in culture. Different cultures use and interpret time and space differently.[4] In Mediterranean cultures, for instance, men tend to stand very close together, frequently touching each other during conversation. In North Atlantic cultures, the appropriate conversational distance is generally about 3 feet—and, in case you hadn't noticed, men seldom touch each other during social conversation except when they shake hands in greeting.

GROUP COMMUNICATION IN CULTURAL PERSPECTIVE

Comparing Communication Norms

Many cultural rules and norms are observed unconsciously and are not thought about until they are ignored or broken. That is, you take the rules and norms of your culture for granted, you typically follow them, and you expect your communication partners to follow them. But when you move from one culture (or from one sub- or co-culture) to another, rules that were taken for granted and behaviors that seemed automatic may become the source of communication difficulties.

In order to better understand (1) the nature of communication rules and norms and (2) the problems that "strangers" to a culture encounter, try your hand at the exercise below.

Spend fifteen to thirty minutes in a familiar environment (preferably your home or dorm) observing the communication behaviors and patterns of those around you from the perspective of a visitor from a different culture. Do not take anything for granted. Do not indicate to your subjects that you are observing their behavior. Conduct your observations with respect for your subjects.

Record the results of your observations, paying special attention to how you understood what was appropriate behavior. Now, ask yourself:

- What rules and norms can I list?
- How did I identify these rules and norms?
- Do they apply to more than one "culture" (that is, are they peculiar to the context I observed or can they be generalized to other, similar contexts)?
- How does my experience compare with those of my classmates?
- Were conflicting or different norms "discovered" by different people from either the same or different "cultures"?
- How would the people around me react if I had violated these norms?
- How could a person from one culture best discover a rule in another culture?
- How can (or should) people from one culture adhere to another culture's rule when that rule violates a rule from their own culture?

COMMUNICATION IS INTENTIONAL

A behavior must be **intentional** to be communicative. If you see me do something or hear me say something I did not intend for you to see or hear, did I communicate with you? Am I responsible to you for what I did or said in the same way as if I had intentionally formulated a message and transmitted it to you? Can you stop yourself from blushing when you don't want to blush?

While communication is sometimes characterized by behavior that is primarily (if not totally) symbolic and intentional and has a cognitive basis, other times our communication is based on emotional and physiological considerations, characterized by a widely shared code that has few, if any, cultural boundaries and is spontaneous.[5] This distinction can be seen as one of *giving* information versus one of *giving off* information.[6] The practical importance of the distinction is that we tend to see a person as more accountable when he or she consciously or purposefully gives information to someone else than when the recipient gleans information from observation or overhearing.

This is not to say that information *given off* is unimportant. In fact, it may be evaluated as more honest because the person giving off the information did not have the opportunity to censor or package it. It is useful to note, however, that while some messages transmitted through the emotional communication system are highly reliable and easily interpreted (e.g., emotional displays like grief and anger), most are ambiguous and open to a variety of interpretations (What does a flushed face mean?). Generally this sort of information can be interpreted through contextual cues, and even then it may be a judgment call that is open to question.

Effective communication requires a sensitivity to the fact that both your intended and unintended messages have an impact on the people around you. Keep in mind that the intended meaning (if there is one) of your behavior is not always as clearly expressed or as accurately received as you would like.

COMMUNICATION IS MEDIATED

Communication requires a **medium**—a vehicle to transport or carry the symbols. In face to face interaction, the vehicle is the air through which the sound and light waves travel. However, communication doesn't need to be face-to-face to be effective; it can be maintained through a variety of media. Long-distance relationships are becoming ever more common. As we move away from face-to-face contact and technology intervenes between us and our **audience**, the characteristics and the social impact of our messages change, sometimes in very subtle ways. With the advent of the information superhighway, which will merge television, cable, telephone, and online computer services in the home, we are likely to see an increase in several types of long-distance relationships. These relationships include not only those between parents and children, siblings, and close friends, but also commuter marriages and even "telecommuting"—arrangements in which the employee is connected to the workplace by computer and audio/video media and so can go to work without leaving home.

COMMUNICATION IS TRANSACTIONAL

Communication is **transactional**; that is, two or more people exchange **sender** and **receiver** roles, and their messages are dependent on and influenced by those of their partner(s). This exchange can be immediate, as in a conversation, or delayed, as in the case of mass media messages or e-mail exchanges.

We have looked at the six major characteristics of communication. Let us now turn our attention to the primary reason for constructing communicative messages in the first place: achieving satisfying relationships in which we can accomplish our personal and group communication goals.

WHAT IS GROUP COMMUNICATION?

Now that we have explored the nature of *communication*, let's take a look at what *group communication* means.

Being a **group** means that people have interdependent relationships with each other. It is these relationships that are the essence of being a group — without the relationships, there is no group! Can people exchanging small talk in an airport terminal or fans cheering at a hockey game be considered a group? While they may *look* like a group, these people don't share a relationship — in other words, they are not sharing sustained, purposeful communication with each other.

ETHICALLY SPEAKING

Your Ethical Responsibility in the Transactional Communication Process

When you engage others in communication, you are not only attempting to influence them in some way, you are also opening yourself to influence by others. We are all involved in the transactional process of communication. Keep in mind that all parties to an interaction are responsible for its outcome and have a hand in whether or not individual and relational goals are met. Whether you are talking with your significant other, a parent, a work group in a class, or the audience of a public speech, you share responsibility for the outcome of the interaction. The burden of responsibility is usually more or less equally distributed, depending on the communication situation. In some situations, like public speaking, the speaker tends to assume most of the responsibility and is seen as the person attempting to influence the audience. But even in this apparently lopsided situation, the audience still retains a good deal of influence. The audience's power is most obvious when applause or catcalls interrupt a speech.

Group communication, then, can be defined as the process of exchanging messages among a collection of people (three or more, and usually not more than twenty) for the purpose of developing a relationship and accomplishing goals.

WHAT ARE THE BENEFITS OF EFFECTIVE GROUP COMMUNICATION?

Groups occupy a large amount of your time and energy while you are a student, and they take up even more of your time afterward. You may participate in as many as twenty conferences or meetings a week if you decide to take a job in a large, complex organization. One estimate has suggested that 82 percent of all U.S. companies use problem-solving and decision-making groups or teams as an integral part of their operations.[7]

Learning how to communicate effectively in groups is one of the most worthwhile investments you can make. Groups are critical to your success, regardless of what kinds of activities you are involved with now or what you might undertake in the future. Groups are so important in modern organizations that they are described as the building blocks for improving effectiveness.[8] If you were the manager or owner of a small business, you would hold frequent staff meetings with your employees. You might be asked to serve on a committee in your place of worship. You may participate in a group designed to prevent crime or improve safety in your neighborhood. Undoubtedly, you will meet some new friends with whom you may go out to eat on a regular basis, thus forming a new informal group.

HOW DOES GROUP COMMUNICATION DIFFER FROM OTHER FORMS OF COMMUNICATION?

Communication between two people—known as **dyadic communication**—is likely the type of communication you encounter most on a day-to-day basis. While both dyadic communication and group communication share the six characteristics of communication that we described earlier, these two forms of communication also differ from each other. The differences between them include:

- The number of people communicating and interacting
- The complexity of the relationships between or among the people who are interacting

Let's take a look at each of the ways that group communication is unique.

GROUP COMMUNICATION MEANS MORE INTERACTANTS

Communication between dyads and groups differs simply because the number of people who are communicating differs. As the number of participants in an interaction increases:

- **The interaction is more formal.** Participants may feel the need to obtain permission to speak; they may limit the length and frequency of their contributions so that other members will not perceive them as dominant; they may be reluctant to interrupt a speaker.

- **Each member has fewer opportunities to contribute.** Participants may want to or be required by a leader to share "floor time" with other group members; time constraints can inhibit the quality and quantity of their contributions.

- **The communication becomes less intimate.** The greater the number of participants, the less comfortable participants feel self-disclosing or voicing controversial opinions.

- **The interaction consumes more time.** As more participants are invited to give input or to debate an idea, the interaction takes longer to complete.

GROUP COMMUNICATION MEANS MORE COMPLEX RELATIONSHIPS

Another factor that separates dyads from groups concerns the complexity of the relationships that the people share. As more participants are added, the

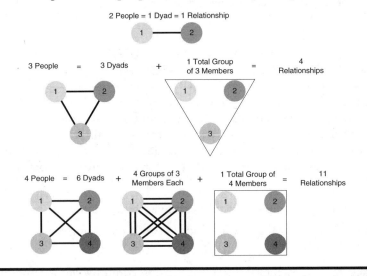

FIGURE 1.1 Each time a person is added to a group, the number of potential relationships increases substantially.

relationships become more complex. In the dyad, of course, there is only one relationship—that between person 1 and person 2. However, in small group communication, there are a myriad of relationships shared between and among the group members, as shown in Figure 1.1.

As you join a group, a couple of points immediately become clear. First, you will not be able to maintain satisfactory relationships with every other member of the group at all times. Over time, you will find evidence of misunderstanding, envy, jealousy, hatred, or possessiveness between any two or more members in the group. Group members do not usually voice these feelings in meetings; instead, they keep them inside in the hope that they will "blow over" with time. Many of these feelings result from quick judgments that are not well founded, and when people see their judgments contradicted by evidence, they often feel guilty.

Second, most groups that function over a period of time develop cliques or coalitions. Cliques or coalitions are formed by individuals who have bonded together in a group.[9] These individuals typically sit next to each other in meetings, take breaks from meetings together, maintain contact with each other outside of meetings, act and think in similar ways, vote together, and support one another's positions.

When **cliques** or **coalitions**—exclusive groups held together by common interests and activities—are present in a group, relationships become more complex because you are no longer dealing only with individuals. Rather, you must maintain relationships with bonded subgroups. You may be able to think of occasions when you were undecided on how to vote on a problem because you did not want to align yourself with one coalition or the other and thereby cause hurt feelings or broken relationships.

2 Participating in Small Group Communication

Groups are only as good as the individuals who participate in them. As such, the quality of any group's work is often determined by the competence that each member of the group brings to any task.

WHAT MAKES A GOOD GROUP MEMBER?

Key competencies for individual success in groupwork include:

- Applying critical thinking
- Making use of attributions
- Monitoring perceptions
- Overcoming communication apprehension

Let's explore each of these characteristics of effective group members.

APPLYING CRITICAL THINKING IN GROUPS

Critical thinking helps you view the world from a reasoned and proactive perspective. Thinking critically requires that you remain open-minded about what you perceive while you inject a healthy dose of inquiry and skepticism into your perceptions. Thus, you have to consider several different viewpoints before you are satisfied with the information you receive. Critical thinkers are always on the lookout for opinions, evidence, or facts that will lead them to accurate and responsible conclusions. This is an extremely important skill that you will want to develop as a group member.

Avoid Critical Thinking Traps
Critical thinkers are less likely to fall into some common traps that plague group communication. As a group member, you should be wary of certain obstacles that are more likely to arise in group communication than in dyadic interactions.[1] Some common traps to avoid are:

- **Accepting communication at face value.** Group members come to rely on and trust one another, and often when time is short, the tendency is to accept communication at face value. This is a serious problem, however, because if communication messages are accepted without question, the issues at hand are not being critically analyzed. Effective group communicators evaluate the worth of everything that is said based on previous discussion and information that the group knows is true. This strategy is designed not to attack others, but to provide a reasoned and logical approach to analyzing what other group members say. Sometimes a simple question is enough to begin an evaluation of someone's comment or argument ("Carol, are you saying that we should just accept these preliminary figures as our data?").

- **Oversimplifying issues.** When groups deal with complex problems, they tend to oversimplify the issues involved. Think about the last time you and a couple of other people had to solve a problem that seemed overwhelming (e.g., travel plans, college costs, a wedding, family problems). Did you notice how some of your partners were willing to oversimplify the issue?

- **Making overgeneralizations.** A conclusion that is taken too far is known as an **overgeneralization**. This trap occurs when one piece of data is assumed to represent all comparable data. For example, if you assume that all teenagers experiment with drugs and alcohol, you are overgeneralizing. Critical thinkers test the validity of a generalization by determining whether the basis of support is biased in any way. A valid generalization is supported by different types of evidence and does not make claims beyond a reasonable point.

- **Making false assumptions.** A conclusion drawn from faulty reasoning is known as a **false assumption**; such assumptions come primarily from inappropriate causal relationships. Sometimes people assume that because two events occurred together or are related, then one must have caused the other. For example, if all males in a class received an A for the course, you might conclude that being male "caused" the grade. However, as is true of most events, numerous factors influenced the grades, such as individual achievement, study habits, related courses, or extra credit assignments. In other words, most events are too complex to establish a single causal-effect relationship. Although it is possible that all males in the class received an A because of gender, it is more likely that individual ability and work "caused" the grades.

Develop Your Critical Thinking Skills

Improving the way you think requires that you develop specific strategies to broaden your abilities. The following strategies will help you develop your skills in critical thinking:

- **Consider multiple perspectives.** Since there is always more than one way to look at things, consider different perspectives and realize that your own perspective is subject to error.

- **Clarify values.** Determine the values that influence your judgment. Understand what your standards are and why you use them.

- **Clarify issues.** Clarify the questions you must answer or the issues with which you must deal. Formulate each issue in a clearly stated sentence.

- **Evaluate information.** Recognize the source of the information. Is it opinion, or is it based on evidence and reasoning? Examine the credibility and relevance of the information.

- **Probe.** Ask searching questions about issues. Look for underlying subjects, ideas, and specific details. Probe for reasons, causes, and alternative views.

- **Identify contradictions.** Recognize significant similarities and differences in opposing views, pinpointing contradictions between opposing arguments.

- **Consider the big picture.** Make plausible inferences and interpretations based on valid information. Explore the implications of statements and develop a fuller, more complete understanding of their meaning.

- **Pursue valid assumptions.** Avoid faulty assumptions based on inappropriate causal relationships.

- **Summarize.** Summarize relevant facts and evidence in clear, understandable statements.

- **Draw appropriate conclusions.** Generate multiple solutions and analyze the feasibility of those solutions.[2]

MAKING USE OF ATTRIBUTIONS IN GROUPS

When you make **attributions**, you assign reasons or causes for another's behavior. Whenever you attempt to explain why someone acts in a certain way or says certain things, you make attributions. Many of your attributions are based on observations of previous behaviors and predispositions, and these can affect your ability as a competent communicator.

Many people believe that making attributions is a normal part of getting to know a person better. As you become more familiar with someone, you begin to think that you are privy to why the person behaves the way he or she does. For example, you see a friend drinking iced tea rather than a cocktail at a party. You may reason that this person is abstaining from alcohol to ensure he will feel fresh for a major presentation you know he is giving very early the next morning. You hear another friend criticize someone's lavish spending. Knowing that this friend grew up in a family with a limited income, you attribute her view to her upbringing. Note that in these two examples, more than a superficial knowledge of the individual is required.

Attributions influence your communication behavior in a group, demonstrating the adage "What you see is what you speak." If you perceive your committee chairperson as competent and intelligent, yet fiercely irritated during a meeting, you are likely to edit your comments and not antagonize this person further. If you attribute the leader's failure to stay organized and follow an agenda for a meeting to the fact that this person has flu symptoms, you may not say the negative things about the leader that you would otherwise say.

MONITORING PERCEPTIONS IN GROUPS

Group members continually form **perceptions** of one another. Perception is the process of making sense of your world. Whenever you engage in a conversation with a group member, you will encounter numerous, specific bits of information — including the exact words of the message, the person's tone of voice, the facial expression, and the presence or lack of eye contact — that may influence your perception.

Perception begins with information you receive from other people. This information can be practically anything — the way people greet you, their clothing, their tone of voice, or even the way they sit in a chair. You can either observe this information yourself or hear about it from others.

Having noted another's behavior, you organize the information and try to make sense of it. In other words, you make an effort to "size" someone up. Even in the briefest encounter you will receive input that will influence your perception of group members and group interaction. As an effective group communicator, you must learn to manage all of this information — to make sense of it all.

Most people form perceptions of others in a matter of seconds. For example, you drive past a twenty-something-year-old male driving a shiny new BMW and think, "spoiled brat." You see a woman sitting in a corner during a talkative party and think, "shy."

Furthermore, most people think their initial perceptions are pretty accurate — yet, how easy it is to be wrong. How do you know that the BMW is his? Maybe the woman in the corner is upset or is attempting to draw attention to herself. In short, you can make many interpretations of another person's behavior, but not all of them will be accurate. Although people are probably not as perceptive as they think they are, in a group context, they rarely have a chance to confirm or deny their perceptions.

OVERCOMING COMMUNICATION APPREHENSION IN GROUPS

A final factor that affects an individual's competence in small groups is communication apprehension. **Communication apprehension** is defined as "fear or anxiety associated with real or anticipated communication with another person or persons."[3] Estimates suggest that about 20 percent of the population is highly apprehensive about communicating.[4]

Think about the times that you have been with a group and felt hesitant or apprehensive about contributing. Can you remember why you felt this way? Can you remember how you felt? Many people who are apprehensive about communicating also experience physiological reactions, such as increased heart rate, sweaty palms, quivering lips, locked knees, or an upset stomach.

Effects of Communication Apprehension in Groups

Simply put, group members who are apprehensive about communicating are likely to be less effective than those who are not. Research into communication apprehension is quite extensive. Generally, highly apprehensive individuals report that this apprehension has a negative effect on many aspects of their lives.[5] Compared to those who are not apprehensive, individuals with high communication apprehension are considered less socially attractive, less competent, less sociable, less composed, and less able to lead. In addition, they are less likely to have high grades in college, to be offered interviews and jobs, or to be satisfied with their subsequent employment. However, there is no indication that they are any less intelligent.

Communication researchers McCroskey and Richmond discuss several results of communication apprehension that are specific to the small group setting.[6] Compared to individuals who are not apprehensive, persons high in communication apprehension are seen in the following ways:

- They are perceived by other group members as being more nervous and less dominant.

- They are perceived as being less task oriented and less socially attractive (because participants are biased in favor of individuals who contribute more frequently in meetings).

- They are seldom perceived as leaders.

- They are perceived as making less valuable contributions to the group.

Assess, Control, and Manage Communication Apprehension

You can become a more effective group communicator by assessing your current abilities and finding out where you stand. You can then move to higher levels of competence. Because apprehension can affect competence, your responses to the checklist "How Well Do You Interact in a Group Setting?" should be helpful to you. If you score high on this checklist, don't worry! Remember, you are in good company; as much as 20 percent of the general population reports the same level of apprehension as you do. You can manage your apprehension in a group in three ways:

- **Use relaxation techniques such as breathing and muscular control.** Taking a deep breath is one of the simplest relaxation tools available to you. You can take several good deep breaths during meetings, and no one will even notice. You will be much less anxious about speaking if you do this.

- **Recognize that part of your apprehension is psychological.** You feel anxiety or fear because of what you think about the situation you are in. Often, telling yourself something like "I'll make a fool of myself if I bring up my view" produces a great deal of anxiety. Such statements are both negative and unfounded, for you have no evidence concerning whether you will or won't make a fool of yourself. If you can replace these types of statements with more realistic ones, such as "Someone here will understand and appreciate my contribution," you will have a more positive attitude and considerably less apprehension.

- **Prepare carefully for a group meeting.** Organize your thoughts into notes; bring any materials needed, such as paper and pens; and summarize any data you want to share with your group. You might want to practice stating your views before the meeting, so that you will be able to explain your ideas as clearly as possible. Remember to *manage* apprehension, not

CHECKLIST

How Well Do You Interact in a Group Setting?

In order to test how apprehensive you might be in a group setting, complete the following six items, which are based on the Personal Report of Communication Apprehension (PRCA-24). Use the following scale:

1 = strongly agree; 2 = agree; 3 = undecided;
4 = disagree; and 5 = strongly disagree.

1. I do not like to participate in group discussions.

2. Generally, I feel comfortable participating in group discussions.

3. I am tense and nervous while participating in group discussions.

4. I like to get involved in group discussions.

5. I get tense and nervous when I engage in a group discussion with new people.

6. I am calm and relaxed while participating in group discussions.

Scoring: Use the following formula, in which the numbers in parentheses represent your answers to the six items. (For example, if you answered "4" for item 1, then replace the "(1)" in the formula with a 4.)

$$18 - (1) + (2) - (3) + (4) - (5) + (6)$$

A score of 24 or above indicates a high level of communication apprehension for participation in group discussions; a score of 12 or below indicates a low level of communication apprehension for this situation.

SOURCE: Adapted from J. C. McCroskey, *An Introduction to Rhetorical Communication,* 4th ed. (Englewood Cliffs, NJ: Prentice-Hall, 1982).

eliminate it, because a small amount of apprehension will actually help you as a communicator.

Individual effectiveness in group communication consists of identifying with the goals of the group and developing critical thinking skills. Individual attributions, perceptions, and apprehension also affect the individual's contribution to group communication. You can use these internal processing components competently if you maintain objectivity and pursue a healthy sense of reality.

WHAT MAKES A GOOD GROUP?

Now that we've discussed the factors that help an individual contribute effectively to a group, let's explore the factors that help the *group itself* achieve success as a collective unit. Key characteristics of a well-functioning group include the development and maintenance of:

- Interdependence among group members
- Cohesion among group members
- Strategies to recognize and avoid groupthink
- An application of productive conflict
- Accepted group norms
- A positive group image

Let's explore each of these characteristics individually.

INTERDEPENDENCE IN GROUPS

A key characteristic of most groups is **interdependence**. Simply put, the behavior of each member affects the behavior of every other member. In most groups today, no member exists in isolation. Many groups are organized with the goal of having their members share tasks.

Products, services, and results from groups with high degrees of interdependence truly belong to the "group" and not to an individual. Words such as we, us, and our are frequently heard in meetings and conversations. Managers who would ordinarily blame a particular person for a problem with a product have difficulty doing so when tasks are completed interdependently. The fault and responsibility, like the credit for successes, are shared among several group members.

A good example of interdependence in groups can be found in most office units. Consider an office with one manager, one secretary, and three staff employees. If the secretary does not distribute mail to the manager and the employees, neither the customers' nor other departmental needs within the organization will be met. If the manager does not work with each employee on scheduling, the work may be distributed unevenly, overburdening one person while allowing another person to slack off. If the employees do not submit their monthly progress reports, the manager will not be able to adequately represent the department in meetings with upper management. In other words, the effectiveness and efficiency of each individual in the work group depend on the effectiveness and efficiency of each of the others.

COHESION IN GROUPS

The "togetherness" of a group is called its **cohesion**. A cohesive group is a tight unit that is able to hang together in the face of opposition. Rosenfeld argues that without cohesion, "individual members are unlikely to commit themselves to the group, the task, or each other, and it is common for undesirable tasks . . . not to get done."[7]

You can determine group cohesion in two ways. First, how do the participants feel about their own membership in the group? The more that members are enthusiastic, identify with the purposes of the group, and tell outsiders about its activities, the more cohesive the group will be.

Second, how well does the group retain its members? The more that members receive satisfaction and fulfill their needs through their group participation, the more cohesive the group. Shaw provides numerous ideas about cohesiveness:

- Member satisfaction is greater in high-cohesive groups than in low-cohesive groups.
- High-cohesive groups exert greater influence over their members than do low-cohesive groups.
- Communication is more extensive and more positive in high-cohesive groups than in low-cohesive groups.
- High-cohesive groups are more effective than low-cohesive groups in achieving goals.[8]

Even the language a group uses can increase its cohesion. Baird and Weinbert argue that as groups succeed and grow, they tend to develop a unique vocabulary.[9] Over time, the words become a code that is practically impossible for an outsider to understand.

Think about how a dentist might use a unique vocabulary in her office. Rather than frightening patients by specifying the names of instruments or drugs used in her procedures, Dr. Hanna communicates to her office staff in code. An assistant may be asked to bring in a "brown 2," standing for Novocain to deaden the mouth. Similarly, "charcoal" is a term used for extraction forceps. The language used in the office among her staff, then, helps to solidify its cohesion.

RECOGNIZING AND AVOIDING GROUPTHINK IN GROUPS

A number of years ago, I. L. Janis coined a term—**groupthink**—to describe situations in which groups strive to reach a consensus and minimize conflict by failing to critically examine ideas, analyze proposals, or test solutions.[10] He argued that groupthink results from strong feelings of loyalty and unity within a group—from too much cohesion. When these feelings are stronger than the desire to evaluate alternative courses of action, a group's decision may be adversely affected. Groups that are prone to groupthink typically exhibit these behaviors:

- Participants reach outward consensus and avoid conflict so as not to hurt others' feelings, even though they may not genuinely be in agreement.
- Members who do not agree with the majority are pressured to conform.
- Disagreement, tough questions, and counterproposals are discouraged.
- More effort is spent justifying decisions than testing them.

The issue of groupthink can generate several ethical considerations.[11] When groupthink causes the ideas, inquiries, and solutions of minority members to be ignored, the group may be acting in an unethical manner. All ideas are important, and the ethical group is one that searches for the best possible set of ideas. When the decision-making moment comes, only those solutions that have met the tests of critical examination and inquiry will be held as most ethical. In many cases, groupthink prevents critical inquiry. In a way, groupthink is a form of censorship because it squelches some members and their ideas. Striving for full participation by all members is a basic tenet of ethical communication.

APPLYING PRODUCTIVE CONFLICT IN GROUPS

When communicative partners hold different positions on an issue, conflict occurs. **Conflict** is defined by communication researchers Hocker and Wilmot as "an expressed struggle between at least two interdependent parties who perceive incompatible goals, scarce rewards, and interference from the other party in achieving their goals."[12]

At many times in your life, you and another person or persons will have conflicting goals, or you will face competition for scarce resources. You will even encounter people who will attempt to thwart your efforts to achieve important goals. Effective group communicators manage, rather than minimize or eliminate, conflict within the groups to which they belong. You may think of managing conflict as bargaining, negotiating, debating, or arguing.

Conflict is a healthy form of group communication when managed properly. Conflict is just as important in group communication as it is in relationships between two people. You already know that issue-based conflict should be fostered. Groups that maximize issue-based conflict and minimize personal-based conflict are the most successful. Leaders and group members should encourage issue-based conflict and remain watchful for instances of personal attacks.

The best of all worlds occurs when group members "agree to disagree." This means that they accept the responsibilities that accompany issue-based conflict. Members know that they will be questioned, second-guessed, and required to defend their positions. They also know that they should not let any issue "slide by" without questioning, pressing other members for clarification and details, or presenting alternative ideas.

ESTABLISHING NORMS IN GROUPS

All kinds of groups develop **norms**, or "sets of expectations held by group members concerning what kind of behavior or opinion is acceptable or unacceptable, good or bad, right or wrong, appropriate or inappropriate."[13] Norms are determined by the group itself and are imposed by members on themselves and each other. Norms can be developed for just about anything a group does, and it is during the first few meetings of a group that they are developed.

Norms direct the behavior of the group as a whole and affect the conduct of individual members. For example, it may be a norm for members to arrive on time (group norm), and it may be a norm for the leader to begin discussion (individual member norm).

In group communication, norms can exist for:

- the kinds of topics that can be expressed in a meeting (Should non-task-related conversation be interjected? Are jokes appropriate?)

- how long someone speaks

- who should speak first (Should the group sit quietly until the leader opens the meeting?)

- negative comments (Is it acceptable to criticize others publicly?)

Group norms such as these affect the communication behavior of any group. The quality and quantity of what is said in a group are often determined by norms.

As a group member, you should be aware of the group's norms, and you should also be prepared to change them if they appear to be detrimental. For example, groups that expect one member to dominate the conversation, criticize ideas before they are analyzed and discussed, or discourage disagreement have norms that are detrimental to communication and goals.

Changing the group's norms can be managed diplomatically:[14]

- **First, establish yourself as a loyal member dedicated to the group.** In this way, you will demonstrate that you have the group's best interest at heart.
- **Second, cite specific examples of the behavior you find harmful to the group's interactions.** You cannot maintain credibility with those you are persuading unless you can back up your claims with specific instances of the norm.
- **Third, calmly state how the norm detracts from the goals of the group and ask for the opinions of the other members.** If the group feels that the norm is warranted, members may offer explanations, thus changing your perception, or the group may decide a change is needed. Whatever the consensus of the group members, they will appreciate your concern, and the group will not suffer undue tension.

THE GROUP IMAGE IN GROUPS

A positive group image may yield several positive outcomes:

- **Success generates success.** Having achieved one goal can motivate a group to "go for more."

GROUP COMMUNICATION IN CULTURAL PERSPECTIVE

Cross-Cultural View of Group Norms

Not all cultures and subcultures view group norms in the same way. For example, political groups in the United States stress open participation by all members but adhere to strict parliamentary procedures when conducting official business. Japanese businesses have adopted norms whereby work groups do not recognize formal lines of authority and status during group meetings.

What about gender norms? What specific norms apply to males and females as they work in groups? What about people who belong to an older generation? Do you think they prefer group norms different from those of younger people?

As part of a group exercise, generate sets of norms that you believe various cultural groups prefer. Interview members of these groups to confirm your expectations. Your group should be prepared to discuss its findings in class.

- **Increased group optimism in the face of obstacles.** A group that has confidence in itself tends to minimize problems, eliminate barriers, and cope well with crises. In these cases, the members believe they cannot be defeated.

- **Special significance to group membership.** Outsiders who are not part of the group frequently aspire to membership or even envy those who have it. People want to be part of groups that are doing well and that are perceived as "on the go." Many groups that achieve momentum after several successful activities find that more people want to join and participate.

Groups can be just as motivated when they are pulling themselves back up on their feet. You can probably think of a number of groups whose very survival was uncertain. If its members perceived the group's existence as worthwhile, you probably saw them "pull together" with hard work to save the group. Teamwork and cooperation are almost always at their highest when group members are in a weak position, set a high performance objective, and work feverishly to achieve that objective.

TECHNIQUES FOR IMPROVING COMMUNICATION IN GROUPS

Although communication is one of the most important functions for a group, that communication is not always efficient, effective, or productive — on many occasions it is of poor quality and undesirable. So how can groups go about improving their communication? Five strategies to improving communication in groups include the use of the following:

- Goal setting
- Agenda setting
- Deliberation and participation
- Roles
- Networks

GOAL SETTING IN GROUPS

Think of the worst group meeting you have ever attended. How would you describe that meeting? Would you say it was "unorganized," "a waste of time," and "unproductive"? Did you wonder why you even spent time meeting with the group? Did you leave the meeting with a bad attitude about working with the group again in the future?

When people have these kinds of reactions, there is generally one underlying problem: the lack of a clear goal. For any organized group, members should know the answer to these questions:

- For what purpose(s) does your group exist?
- Do all group members understand and accept the goals? Are they committed to them?
- How close is your group to achieving its goals?
- How well are your group's activities or functions aligned with the goals?

Goals vary considerably depending on the type of group involved. For example, a group in one of your classes may have the simple goal of completing a fifteen-minute, in-class exercise and reporting the results to the rest of the class. Your volunteer group at a rape crisis center may have the goal of providing quality assistance to rape survivors. An urban beautification fund-raising committee for underprivileged families may have the goal of collecting $4,000 for neighborhood housing improvements by auctioning off a donated entertainment system.

Your major responsibility as a leader is to keep the group "on course," ensuring that its work is aligned with its goal. The more that you keep the group's goal as a benchmark from which to monitor your own activities, the better organized and the more efficient you will be.

CHECKLIST

A Group Leader's Strategies for Effective Goal Setting

If you have a leadership role in a group, you should be a catalyst in setting group goals. You may either set the goals yourself or work with the group in establishing goals. The second option is preferable because group members are likely to be more committed and excited about a goal that they have helped create. How can you do this?

✓ **Identify the problem.** Specify what is to be accomplished or completed.

✓ **Map out a strategy.** Determine the desired performance level and a means to evaluate whether the level has been attained.

✓ **Set a performance goal.** Recognize the group's capabilities and limitations and establish a realistic target.

✓ **Identify the resources necessary to achieve the goal.** Needed time, equipment, and money are among the important issues to consider before beginning.

✓ **Obtain feedback.** Prepare to adjust directions or methods if necessary so that the group is doing its best.

SOURCE: Dan O'Hair and Gustav W. Friedrich, *Strategic Communication in Business and the Professions* (Boston: Houghton Mifflin, 1992).

As a group member, you should evaluate proposals, decisions, or other activities in light of your group's goal. You may sometimes have to resist going along with the majority or becoming emotional during a meeting. The more you use the group's goal to guide you, the more satisfied you are likely to be as a participant.

AGENDA SETTING IN GROUPS

An agenda is to a group what a city map is to a tourist or a compass is to a sailor. Without these aids, people are likely to flounder aimlessly, waste time, and solve problems inefficiently. Agendas are more than simple outlines that a group leader follows while presiding over a meeting. Typically, at the top of an agenda is the name of the group, the meeting place, and the anticipated time span. This is followed by a list of topics and subtopics that will be covered during the meeting. Many agendas include the name of the person who is primarily responsible for each topic and a time frame for each presentation. An agenda usually looks like the model shown in Figure 2.1.

A group leader should always prepare an agenda before a meeting. This does not mean, however, that the group must adhere to it rigidly. Many group leaders distribute an agenda to participants and then ask if anyone has an item to add. During the course of a meeting, if the leader feels that a topic that is scheduled for discussion later should be dealt with at the present time, he or she can make those adjustments.

ETHICALLY SPEAKING

Balancing Group Goals with Personal Goals

How do you balance group goals with personal goals? Think of a situation in which your personal goals were in conflict with a group's goals. Did group members try to convince you to adjust your own goals for the sake of the group? Did you attempt to change the group's goals to accommodate your own? Is it always right to subordinate personal goals to group goals or vice versa? Does it depend on the situation? As you read the following scenario, imagine yourself in the situation and consider the ethical issues involved.

At the advertising agency where you are a copywriter, you are assigned to a tobacco account. You are opposed to the advertising and promotion of smoking. The only way you can resign from the account is to resign from your job. If you stay on, how can you make a professional, conscientious effort to create effective advertising copy and still stay true to your beliefs about smoking?

Cleveland Engineering Society
Petroleum Club, Room 224
Thursday, November 14, 2004
4:30–6:30 P.M.

   I. Call to Order (1 min.)   Jane Winer, President

  II. Roll Call (1 min.)   Jane Winer, President

 III. Reading of Minutes (3 min.)   Ralph Sikewa, Secretary

 IV. Financial Report   Barry Jefferson, Treasurer

  V. Old Business

   October meeting (5 min.)

   Volunteer update (10 min.)   Viola Florez-Cantu, Volunteer Chair

 VI. New Business

   December meeting (10 min.)   Randy Sato, Program Chair

   Scholarship progress (10 min.)

   Christmas party (10 min.)

   Guidelines for ethics document
   (30 min.)

 VII. Announcements

VIII. Adjournment

**FIGURE 2.1 A printed agenda typically follows the format of the model
shown here.**

The key advantage of using an agenda is that the leader and all participants can know where the group has been and where it is going. With an agenda, it is only minimally possible that a group will omit a key discussion point.
An agenda helps ensure that a meeting is orderly, efficient, and organized.

DELIBERATION AND PARTICIPATION IN GROUPS

Certainly, not all members of a group are equal; they have different backgrounds, ethnicity, experiences, education, biases, skills, competence, and
interests. Therefore, to say that all members of a group should participate
equally on all topics is impractical and detrimental to its effectiveness.

Yet sometimes group members do not participate when their contributions would be beneficial. Even participants who are highly qualified in a

particular area sometimes choose not to do so. Why? Let's look at a few reasons for nonparticipation.

- **Apprehension.** Members may experience fear or anxiety about expressing themselves in the group.
- **Lack of self-esteem.** Members may doubt the worth of their contributions.
- **Dominance.** Other group members may control the "floor."
- **Status differences.** Group members who are lower in their political or hierarchical position may choose not to comment on stances taken by superiors in the group.

Research indicates that an imbalance of participation in a group will present problems. A study by Hoffman and Maier found that the solution adopted in a group is the one that receives the largest number of favorable comments.[15] Furthermore, most of those comments come from a single member! However, if the "dominating" group member has inaccurate or incomplete information or less than an optimal solution, the group may make a faulty decision.

ROLES IN GROUPS

Group members can have clearly identifiable roles. A person's **role** is the function that member performs in the group. Words like leader, dominator, gatekeeper, joker, and analyzer are examples of roles in a group.[16]

CHECKLIST

Strategies for Encouraging Group Participation

Groups can use several techniques to encourage participation:

✓ **Ask "gatekeeping" questions.** By asking a member to contribute ("Carolyn, we haven't heard from you yet." "Doug, what do you think about this?"), a leader can directly influence involvement.

✓ **Divide participants into smaller groups for a collective response.** Group members who are reluctant to participate in the larger group can be encouraged or even obligated to provide input in a subgroup containing one or two other members. The leader may want to have each subgroup report the results of its discussion.

✓ **Consult the nonparticipants privately.** A leader may discover why an individual is not participating by simply remarking, "You haven't said much today. Is something wrong?" This method allows the leader to identify and eliminate any obstacles to the quiet member's participation.

Types of Group Roles

In most groups, each member performs or contributes to two basic functions: task and personal roles.

Task roles are concerned with the accomplishment of the goals, objectives, or mission of the group. They are based on the content and substance of the group's interaction, apart from the members' personalities or personal characteristics. Elective offices in organizations and job titles in business firms indicate task roles. Other examples of task roles include:

- **Information giver.** Offers facts, beliefs, personal experience, or other input.

- **Information seeker.** Asks for additional input or clarification of ideas or opinions that have been presented.

- **Elaborator.** Offers further clarification of points, often providing information about what others have said.

- **Initiator.** Helps the group get moving by proposing a solution, giving new ideas, or providing new definitions of an issue.

- **Administrator.** Keeps people on track and aware of the time.

Personal roles are concerned with the relationships among group members. Some people call these roles socioemotional because they are not task related. Individuals who fill these roles help maintain the group as an operating whole. The following are a few examples of this type of role:

- **Harmonizer.** Seeks to smooth over tension in the group by settling differences among members.

- **Gatekeeper.** Works to keep each member involved in a discussion by keeping communication channels open; may restrict information during periods of overload.

- **Sensor.** Expresses group feelings, moods, or relationships in an effort to recognize the climate and capitalize on it.

Every member in a group plays personal as well as task roles. Often, the behaviors that accompany a role are prescribed or assigned; you expect people who assume certain roles to use particular behaviors. In other cases, you learn the roles people play only by observing their behaviors.

How Roles Evolve in Groups

Roles can evolve in two ways. The first way is to consider a position in a group and think of the behaviors you expect the person filling that position to perform. For instance, if there is an elected secretary of your group, you will expect that person to attend meetings, read and take minutes, distribute correspondence, write letters, and make phone calls. You may expect a chairperson to call meetings to order, set an agenda, introduce visitors, facilitate interaction among the members, summarize the proceedings, and so forth.

Second, roles can evolve by observing someone's behavior and then placing a label on that behavior. For example, if a group member is always the first to speak on every topic, cuts others off, and uses an exorbitant amount of "floor time," you might label that person a dominator. Another member who is always prepared with statistics, facts, and evidence might be the information giver.

Identifying and Overcoming Problems with Group Roles

Two kinds of problems arise concerning roles in groups. The first, **role conflict**, exists whenever competing expectations for your behavior are incompatible. A good example would be the leader of a group whose role is "friend" with many members but who must also be an "evaluator" of their performance. If you were the leader, the friendship role would require you to be subjective and kind and to give other people the benefit of the doubt. At the same time, the evaluator role would require you to be objective, impartial, and governed by rules or policies. Experiencing role conflict is one of the most uncomfortable feelings you can have as a group member.

The second problem is the existence of **antigroup roles**. These roles consist of behaviors that attempt to satisfy individual rather than group needs, which are often irrelevant to the task at hand and are clearly not aimed at maintaining the group as a team. How many times have you seen evidence of these antigroup roles in the groups you belong to?

- **Blocker.** Indulges in negative and stubbornly resistant behavior, including disagreements and groundless opposition to ideas; reintroduces an issue after the group has rejected or bypassed it.

- **Avoider.** Displays noninvolvement in the group's proceedings by such behaviors as pouting, cynicism, nonchalance, or "horseplay."

- **Recognition seeker.** Calls attention to himself or herself by behavior such as boasting, providing information about his or her qualifications, or reporting personal achievements.

- **Distractor.** Goes off on tangents or tells irrelevant stories.

NETWORKS IN GROUPS

Still another factor that has a profound effect on group interaction is its networks. **Networks** are defined as the communication patterns used within a group. In essence, you are asking questions such as "Who speaks to whom?" "How often?" and "About what?"

Two key positions typically are important in describing networks in a group. The first is **centrality**, or the degree to which an individual sends and receives messages from others in the group. The most central person in the group receives and sends the highest number of messages in a given time period. You probably believe that leaders of discussion groups or managers of employee teams occupy highly centralized positions because of their status or power. If a leader calls on you to speak in a group, all communication will flow directly through that leader. Therefore, the leader occupies a highly centralized position in the group's network.

Another key position is **isolation**. Relative to others in the group, isolates receive and send fewer messages. You may believe that these are "thinkers" who keep their thoughts to themselves and are not very interested in socializing or interacting with others. In some groups, members are isolates because they are not liked or perceived as competent by the other participants. In other groups, isolates choose to comment very selectively. You should note that both isolation and centrality are highly dependent on the content that is being communicated.

Several types of content-based networks are possible:

- **Innovation networks.** Networks in which participants communicate about new ideas and directions.

- **Social networks.** Networks in which participants discuss nonwork issues, including gossip.

- **Task networks.** Networks that are defined by the job or work at hand or giving technical advice to another person.

A person can be very centralized in one network and yet be practically isolated in another. You may find many examples of this situation. Think for a moment about a group or committee of which you have been a member. Is the individual in your group who contributes and is asked the most about task functions the same person who also contributes the most and is asked the most about social activities? Probably not. You will likely find that the people who are particularly centralized in social networks are popular, outgoing, likable, and so forth. Highly centralized individuals in task networks are likely to be experienced, educated, and competent. In innovation networks, highly centralized persons are usually "insiders" with access to resources, information, and influential people.[17]

If you want to be more centralized in a group, you need to become more visible. Prepare some relevant and thought-provoking comments ahead of time. Speak up. Challenge members' ideas. Ask questions. If you first increase the number of contributions you make in a group, people will then direct comments to you as well. Depending on the quality of your contributions, you could move from an isolate to a central position rather swiftly.

We have discussed several ways that group communication can be improved. Goal setting and agenda setting are both essential. It is also important that all group members contribute through deliberation and participation. Another key is having group members assume roles that directly contribute to group competence while minimizing roles that distract from the group's effectiveness. In addition, members need to be aware of the networks that exist so that centrality is encouraged for all group members.

SPECIAL GROUP TYPES AND TECHNIQUES

Two types of groups meet in ways that deviate from the norm and have purposes that are different from those discussed in the earlier parts of the chapter. They are:

- the nominal group technique
- self-managing teams

Let's take a look at each.

THE NOMINAL GROUP TECHNIQUE

Ironically, the nominal group technique is not a group process at all. Rather, the **nominal group technique** is a process used by individuals working alone in a group context (interaction among participants is not allowed). It is used to produce a basis for discussion that reflects the views of all the group members.

Assume that you are chairperson of a special student committee designed to recruit majors for the various departments in the School of Arts and Sciences. At a meeting, an idea was proposed to conduct a three-hour "open house," with all faculty and majors available to visit with prospective students. You and several group members are not certain this is the best course of action; therefore, as chairperson, you have decided to put the idea to a test using the nominal group technique.

To use this technique, you first ask each member to make a separate listing of the advantages and disadvantages of the proposal. After about fifteen minutes, you call time, and you ask each member to contribute one of his or her advantages or disadvantages. You write each advantage and disadvantage on a flip-chart or transparency as it is mentioned, eliminating any that are repetitious. When the content of everyone's list is exhausted, you proceed to the next step. Ask the participants to copy the master list on a sheet of paper. You then announce that, as individuals, they are to rank order each advantage and disadvantage from highest to lowest in priority. The lists are submitted to you. You might ask the group to take a break for a few minutes while you tabulate the priorities for the entire group. When the group reconvenes, you can select the top advantages and disadvantages of the issue to discuss.

Of course, "advantages/disadvantages" is only one of many possible topics for the nominal group technique. You may wish to pose a question and use the technique to brainstorm in a group. For example, you might ask, "What criteria should we use to distribute our scholarship money next year?" If this is the purpose, ideas are brainstormed, listed on a chart, prioritized, and then discussed.

After the discussion, participants select five ideas that are attractive to them, write them on a 3 x 5 card, and then assign a priority ranking to them.

The cards are collected, rank ordered in front of the participants, and a final vote is taken for the best idea. Using e-mail capabilities, this selection of priorities can be accomplished prior to the meeting.

The nominal group technique is recommended when feelings of intimidation, domination, hesitancy, or apprehension surface in a group. Because each participant submits information simultaneously and anonymously, all input is weighted equally prior to the discussion. The technique is also useful when the group does not have a history from which to work. One study even indicated that four-person nominal groups outperformed four-person actual groups and individual groups on anagram tasks.[18]

SELF-MANAGING TEAMS

One of the newest trends concerning small groups in modern organizations is the development of **self-managing teams**—teams consisting of highly skilled workers who are completely responsible for producing high-quality, finished work. Whether the work involves manufacturing, such as a mahogany china cabinet, or a service, such as a financial statement, the result is always the product of a fully integrated team. Members of the team share responsibility for each step of the process, as opposed to a single, narrow individual function, such as would be found on an assembly line.[19] According to Dumaine, one-half of surveyed Fortune 500 companies plan to implement these teams in the future.[20]

Self-managing work teams are actually an outgrowth of two major lines of thought. In the 1960s and early 1970s, participative management became very popular. In this style of management, supervisors would involve themselves with their subordinates in making decisions that were properly labeled group efforts. Supervisors would guide and facilitate discussions and problem-solving sessions but would not impose their decisions on the group. Rather, supervisors worked with their group to jointly address a problem.

In the late 1970s and early 1980s, participative management gave way to **quality circles** in many organizations. Quality circles were groups of employees from the same work area who met on a voluntary basis on company time to analyze and solve work-related problems. The meetings were led by an experienced manager, and participative decision making was used. Quality circles were popular because organizations were able to save large amounts of time and money by allowing employees, who were closest to and most knowledgeable about their jobs, to make recommendations on how to improve the effectiveness and efficiency of work processes. The circles would present their findings to management, who would often enthusiastically consider, endorse, and implement the ideas.

Note that in both models the supervisor is still the focus. In participative management, a supervisor guides and facilitates the meetings; and in quality circles, a supervisor leads the meetings. In self-managing work teams, however, many of the typical management functions are completely controlled by the team members. Employees who are part of these teams arrange their own schedules; buy their own equipment; and set their own standards for productivity, quality, and costs. They conduct their own peer evaluations, hire new members, and coordinate future plans with management. As a result, members have positive attitudes and are committed to the group.

While self-managing teams don't "work as they please," the organizational structure of self-managing teams encourages some of the following positive characteristics:

- A clear sense of their own separate identity
- The alignment of their activities with corporate objectives
- A sense of accountability for their activities
- Conformity to fiscal, legal, and other critical guidelines[21]

Perhaps the most dramatic effect of self-managing teams on the workplace involves the attitudes and skills of the workers. A competitive work environment often changes to one of cooperation. Work in isolation changes to work with others. Managers training employees changes to employees training their peers.

EVALUATING COMPETENCE IN GROUP COMMUNICATION

Two methods of evaluating groups are valid and helpful. First, individual member competence is evaluated by how well members accomplish their roles, how well they control their apprehension levels, how well they participate, and how accurate their perceptions and attributions are. In determining individual competence, it is important for members of the group to practice critical thinking skills. The best group decisions are made when members consider several different perspectives before being satisfied with the information they receive.

Second, groups can be evaluated as to how well they fulfill the functions of communication—namely, control, affiliation, and goal orientation. A group functions in a competent manner when there is general agreement by members as to the distribution of control, the amount of affiliation, and the goals of the group. Finally, competent groups are those that encourage productive conflict and critical thinking to arrive at the best decisions and minimize the extent of groupthink.

3 Leadership and Decision Making in Groups and Teams

THE ROLE OF LEADERSHIP IN GROUP COMMUNICATION

Have you ever thought about the designs of conference tables? What types of decisions are made at a meeting using an oval table? What kind of leader was King Arthur, head of the knights of the round table? In corporations, why are most Japanese and American conference tables rectangular? Now that you've learned the basics of small group communication, let's continue our discussion by examining two essential and interrelated dimensions of communication: group leadership and decision making. These two processes work together to produce valuable group outcomes. As such, it is difficult to discuss one of these processes without discussing the other.

WHAT IS LEADERSHIP?

Think of the last group you were in. What was the leader like? Was he or she effective? How would you define the effective traits of this leader? Over the years, countless attempts have been made to define leadership. In this section, we review some of the basic characteristics of leadership and discuss how different styles work in different groups.

Leadership can be defined as the exercise of interpersonal influence toward the attainment of goals. Two key terms appear in many definitions of leadership — **direction** and **influence**. Many people believe that a leader's primary function is to provide direction. For example, communication researchers Hemphill and Coons note that leadership is the "behavior of an individual when he [or she] is directing the activities of a group toward a shared goal."[1] Stogdill suggests that leadership is the "initiation and maintenance of structure in expectation and interaction."[2] Viewed in this way, leaders structure, guide, and facilitate a group's activities and interaction in ways that will lead to a desired outcome.

Other definitions of leadership focus on influence, and scholars recognize the role of communication in influence. For example, consider these definitions of leadership:

- "Interpersonal influence, exercised in a situation, and directed, through the communication process, toward the attainment of a specified goal or goals."[3]

- "An interaction between persons in which one presents information of a sort and in such a manner that the other becomes convinced that his [or her] outcomes . . . will be improved if he [or she] behaves in the manner suggested or desired."[4]

These definitions highlight the notions that leaders have an impact on other group members and that people who can influence others become leaders. Frequently, group members are influenced by the leader's status or power. In other cases, the influence comes from the group members' admiration or respect for the leader.

TYPES OF LEADERSHIP

Leaders of groups typically exhibit one of four decision-making styles:

- authoritarian
- consultative
- participative
- laissez-faire

Each of these styles has its own unique advantages and disadvantages.

Authoritarian leadership is characterized by the exercise of control by the leader without input from other group members. In most instances, the leader makes a decision and simply communicates it to the group. Although this style produces faster decisions, it has been shown to result in lower group member satisfaction and commitment to the task.

Consultative leadership bases decisions upon the opinons or ideas of group members. This type of leader asks others for their opinions or ideas

CHECKLIST

Characteristics of An Authoritarian Leader

✓ Provides opinions and input but does not actively solicit them from members.

✓ Announces decisions rather than opens them for discussion.

✓ Maximizes upward and downward interaction (leader to member; member to leader) while minimizing lateral interaction (member to member).

✓ Resolves conflicts when they arise.

✓ Groups led by this style of leader are likely to have shorter meetings.

and then makes the final decision alone after considering this input. Leaders use this style when they lack the necessary information to make an effective decision.

Subordinates often find consultative leadership to be a frustrating style, because they see it as a facade the leader uses to make them believe that they are involved. In fact, they claim, very little that they suggest is ever achieved or implemented. Many subordinates wish the leader would not ask them for input in the first place! Nonetheless, leaders often use this style quite constructively to gather information and to test the waters before making a decision. This approach permits a more reasoned and educated outcome.

Participative leadership involves a leader working with other group members to achieve a desired goal. This leadership style is used by leaders who work together with a group in solving a problem or performing a task. The leader typically guides and facilitates but has no more influence over the outcome than does any other group member. Although the decisions made take longer to reach, they typically are of higher quality, result in greater satisfaction, and elicit greater commitment than do decisions made by any other leadership style.

The **laissez-faire leadership** style involves little or no direct leadership. The group simply proceeds with the task. According to communication researcher Bass, "The satisfaction of followers will be lower under laissez-faire leadership than under autocratic leadership if the latter is nonpunitive, appropriate for the followers' levels of competence, or in keeping with the requirements of the situation. Most often, laissez-faire leadership has been consistently found to be the least satisfying and effective management style."[5]

A laissez-faire leader is one who, according to subordinates, stays out of the way, is difficult to find when there is a problem, communicates the absolute

CHECKLIST

Characteristics of a Participative Leader

✓ Asks "gatekeeping" questions to involve nonparticipating members.

✓ Summarizes discussions for group clarity.

✓ Gives his or her own input and ask members for more.

✓ "Harmonizes" discussions that may involve personal conflict.

✓ Announces a problem and opens it for discussion rather than announces a solution.

✓ Encourages all-channel participation, wherein communication flows laterally, upward, and downward.

minimum for members to do their job, and if not bothered, won't bother the group.

Once a leadership style has been established, it can be very difficult to alter, as illustrated in the following story.

The veteran manager in a large corporation attended a three-day seminar on participative leadership during which this style was described. At the end of the seminar, he decided to give it a try. At the next staff meeting, he called everyone together, sat down, and described a problem. Instead of dictating a decision, he asked what everyone believed should be done. They sat there in silence. He asked again. Still they sat there without saying a word. He asked specific staff members. They were speechless. In their minds, they were thinking, "Has he been drinking?" "What's happened to him?"

What do you think this manager did? He went back to his authoritarian behaviors. Why? Because the group forced him to! When he tried to be participative and the group failed to participate, he had to use authoritarian behaviors to get the job done. Thus, just because your mind is set on a particular way to behave does not always mean you will be able to do so. Circumstances may require you to employ behaviors that you had no intention of using.

SHARED LEADERSHIP

Effective small groups share leadership among their members. **Shared leadership** is leadership that emerges from any interested and talented group members, depending upon the context at hand.

How many times have you seen that genuine leadership actually comes from someone other than the person who is the "head" of the group? In reality, the organized manager with well-set agendas may not be nearly as useful to a group as the well-informed subordinate.

A variety of situations permit shared leadership. Consider a city council group faced with making a difficult decision about where to build a new park and how much money to spend. The group is flooded with data; among other things, the members already have bids from contractors, maps, and expert testimonies. At some point, the members "wave a white flag." They do not need any more information. Fortunately, a group member emerges as a leader because that person can organize the group's information. This leader has the uncanny knack of sorting, classifying, or discarding data, and emerges as the leader because organization is what the group needs most at the present time.

Conversely, consider a task force at a department store whose responsibility is to recommend a security system to senior management. Although all members are enthusiastic about participating, only one person has insight into the store's past problems, types of systems, contact firms, and so forth. In all likelihood, this member will emerge as the group leader because she has the information the group needs at that time.

Heads of groups who encourage and facilitate shared leadership are more likely to be effective. When the talents of each individual in a group are brought out and applied, members are likely to be more motivated and the group's needs are more likely to have "all bases covered."

Many businesses and professional organizations in the United States are moving toward a shared leadership model. This means giving people who work at the lower levels of the organization decision-making and leadership responsibilities.

EFFECTIVE LEADERSHIP

Regardless of whether one directs or influences followers, the major criterion should be how well the leader functions, performs, or behaves. **Effective leadership** — credible behavior by which an individual inspires and motivates group members to achieve desirable group outcomes through interaction — may be authoritarian (although this is rarely the case), consultative, participative, or laissez-faire. An effective leader may share leadership in a group and ensure that his or her style is a good match for the group. The important issue is that a leader exhibit effective leadership and communication in leading the group toward desirable results.

Three factors are important for effective leadership:

- **Brings about desirable outcomes.** The outcomes need not be pre-planned or even consistent with previously established goals. The out-

GROUP COMMUNICATION IN CULTURAL PERSPECTIVE

Culture and Shared Leadership

How receptive to shared leadership are the various cultural groups to which you belong? Examine some of the cultures or co-cultures with which you identify — for example, your ethnic group, your gender, your religious affiliation, and your age group.

On a sheet of paper, draw a horizontal line representing a continuum from authoritarian leadership at one end to shared leadership at the other. Place the leadership style common to each of your cultures/groups on the continuum. Does the style change in either direction for groups in which all the members share a cultural identity? What about groups that also include other cultures? For example, is the leadership style of groups whose members are all about the same age different from that of groups in which some members are older or younger?

When you observe the leadership styles that seem most comfortable for your cultural groups, this may facilitate reaching group goals.

comes must, however, be successful, productive, or beneficial for the group. Because outcomes are heavily influenced by the group process, leaders must be able to move the process toward a successful conclusion.

- **Enhances credibility with the group.** Credibility is typically assessed through reactions to questions such as "How knowledgeable is the leader?" "How experienced is the leader?" "How believable is the leader?" or "How much do I respect the leader?" Maybe the members do not like the leader personally, but they believe nonetheless that the person is an effective leader for the group. In that case, the leader certainly has credibility.

- **Inspires and motivates group members to participate.** In some cases, the leader must be a cheerleader for the group. In other cases, an individual may lead by example. In still other instances, the leader may offer tangible rewards that encourage group members to try to achieve.

The three factors we have mentioned are criteria by which to assess how well or what a leader does. Effective leadership is credible behavior by which an individual inspires and motivates group members to achieve desirable group outcomes through interaction.

FACTORS INFLUENCING DECISION MAKING IN GROUPS AND TEAMS

Making decisions with others in a group or a team is a complex process—one you have no doubt already experienced. Factors that affect the process of decision making in groups include:

- Understanding the variables involved in group decision making
- Developing group decision-making skills
- Clarifying group values and goals
- Managing group expectations
- Dealing with time pressures
- Working through conflict

Let's look at each of these factors in detail.

UNDERSTANDING THE VARIABLES AFFECTING GROUP DECISION MAKING

Group decisions are never made in a vacuum. No matter what topic is under discussion, several factors can influence the attitudes and behaviors of individual group members, the climate of the group as a whole, and the final decision. To illustrate how multiple decision-making factors can interact with each other, consider this example.

One of the worst disasters of our time occurred as a result of poor group decision making. On January 28, 1986, the space shuttle *Challenger* exploded 92 seconds after takeoff, killing all seven of its crew members. NASA officials had decided to launch the shuttle even though they had received information that cast doubt on the safety of the mission.

In an analysis of the decision making that led to this tragedy, Hirokawa, Gouran, and Martz argue that three forces influenced the faulty decision.[6] These same forces operate in practically any type of group decision making. They are cognitive, psychological, and social forces.

Cognitive Forces

Cognitive processes are mental, referring to what someone thinks, believes, or feels. They specifically involve the beliefs individuals hold and the methods they use to make decisions. They influence "the manner in which group members attend to, make sense of, and utilize available information" to make decisions.[7]

Cognitive forces include the perception, interpretation, evaluation, storage, retrieval, and integration of information input to an individual. The outcome of any group decision can be greatly affected by the way group members interpret information.

A government commission's investigation of the *Challenger* disaster found that cognitive forces had influenced the NASA officials who made the decision to launch the shuttle. The officials discounted the credibility of key negative information that was available to them at the time. The decision makers also used questionable reasoning to draw incorrect conclusions from the data. Finally, they held faulty beliefs about the shuttle system, which led them to have unwarranted confidence in its ability to launch correctly.

Psychological Forces

Psychological forces refer to the personal motives, goals, attitudes, and values of group members. In the *Challenger* example, two psychological forces influenced the participants' decision making: perceived pressure and a criterion shift.

Lower-level NASA decision makers felt pressure to reverse their earlier recommendation to postpone the launch. Initially, the group had recommended that the launch be postponed until the temperature was higher. That decision was later reversed in the face of strong opposition from higher management officials.

The decision makers also shifted the criterion for postponing the launch. Ordinarily, NASA officials employ a rule that a launch should not take place if there is any doubt of its safety. With this rule, the burden of proof is on the safety of the launch. In this case, officials shifted to a rule suggesting that a launch should proceed unless there is conclusive evidence that it is unsafe to do so. With this rule, the burden of proof is on the risk of the launch. Because risk is always harder to prove than safety, the NASA officials used an incorrect decision criterion as a basis for proceeding with the launch.

Social Forces

Social forces are communicative influences such as language use and persuasion. These forces are present whenever two or more people interact with each other. In the *Challenger* disaster, responsible engineers were unable to persuade their own management and higher NASA officials to postpone the launch. They tried, unsuccessfully, to prove that it was unsafe to launch rather than take the tactic that no data were available to prove that it was safe to launch the *Challenger*. The government commission's investigation also revealed that much ambiguous and confusing language was communicated among various officials.

How do these same forces operate in groups that you work with each day? Think about this point. Have your strongly held beliefs ever caused you to

ETHICALLY SPEAKING

Ethics and O-Rings

Many experts have characterized the *Challenger* disaster as a "communication breakdown." Several communication problems contributed to the space shuttle explosion. Besides the psychological, cognitive, and social variables at work in this situation, it has been suggested that a number of ethical communication issues were involved.* In testimony during the hearings investigating the disaster, we learned that engineers for the O-ring manufacturer Thiokol were very vocal in their objections to the launch of the space shuttle in cold weather. After management overruled their objections and authorized the launch, the engineers were unhappy but silent. If they really believed that people's lives would be in danger, didn't they have a moral and ethical obligation to communicate their concerns to others in positions of authority?

For example, would it have been ethical for the engineers to go over their bosses' heads to even higher authorities? Would it have been ethical for the engineers to talk to the media about their fears? On the other hand, don't decision makers such as the Thiokol engineers have a moral duty to support their superiors' decisions? Going over a boss's head or leaking information to the press is a good way to get fired. Didn't the engineers have an ethical obligation to themselves and their families to keep their jobs?

*See J. A. Jaksa and M. S. Pritchard, *Communication Ethics: Methods of Analysis*, 2nd ed. (Belmont, CA: Wadsworth, 1994).

dismiss contrary information as unimportant or incorrect? Have you ever felt pressure to "go along with the crowd" as part of the decision-making process? Have you always insisted on understanding exactly what others meant before you would agree to a particular conclusion? Most people would answer "yes" to all three of these questions. In the *Challenger* disaster, the loss was greater than seven lives. What will be the cost of your group's next decision?

DEVELOPING GROUP DECISION-MAKING SKILLS

Different people, of course, have different decision-making skills. What is involved when you make any of the following decisions as an individual?

> whether to drop or continue a course you are currently struggling in

> whether to sacrifice now by juggling school and work in order to benefit later with a better, more rewarding job

> whether to eat a light lunch today so that you can feast tonight without guilt at an all-you-can-eat seafood buffet

> whether to accept a job promotion and relocate to another city

For any of these decisions — as well as other ones — you would probably use these processes:

- delineate the alternatives clearly
- decide how distinct the alternatives are
- analyze the "state of affairs" for each alternative
- determine what criteria are the most important for you in making the decision
- using those criteria, conduct a cost/benefit or pro/con analysis for each alternative
- come to a conclusion and make the decision you think is right
- evaluate it later

These same processes, and more, are present when individuals meet as a group to make a decision. Just as some people are better than others at decision making, some groups are better at it as well. In this section we look specifically at group decision-making skills. We discuss four group skills:

- **Analysis.** Analysis refers to "taking apart" a problem and examining its components. When a group conducts an analysis, it probes for sources, causes, effects, and influences.
- **Perspective.** The perspective a group brings to a problem influences its decision-making process in several different ways. How important is the

problem? How many people does it affect? How much money might a particular decision save or cost? How much time should be spent on the issues? Groups that put a problem in proper perspective are better at decision making than those that do not.

- **Focus.** Can the group keep its focus on its task? Or does it get lured into subissues or topics that are irrelevant to the problem at hand? It is easier than you think to move away from the problem under discussion, especially when some group members have partisan agendas. Leaders and group members must be vigilant in keeping the group focused on its primary goal.

- **Summarizing.** Summarizing is very important and should occur with regularity. Summary statements allow group members to assess "where they are" on a given decision. When these statements are voiced with clarity, participants have the opportunity to confirm, correct, or clarify what has occurred up to a certain point. While some people believe that leaders should provide summaries, any participant can attempt to summarize the discussion at any point.

CLARIFYING GROUP VALUES AND GOALS

Before a group proceeds to make decisions, it should engage in values and goals clarification. Simply put, **values** help a group determine whether a decision is right or wrong; **goals** are the ultimate purposes for which decisions are made.

Values

The noted psychologist Rokeach defined a value as "an enduring belief that a specific mode of conduct or end-state of existence is personally or socially preferable to an opposite or converse mode of conduct or end-state of existence."[8] When groups express the idea that certain behaviors are right or wrong or that certain end-states are desirable or undesirable, they are operating from their values. Values significantly affect a group's decision-making process.

For example, U.S. congressional committees hold the value that democracy is preferable to dictatorship. Mothers Against Drunk Driving (MADD) has clearly sent the value-laden message that drinking alcoholic beverages before operating an automobile is very dangerous. Consumer advocacy groups suggest that safety in the manufacture of products is preferable to risk. Raters for the Motion Picture Association of America (MPAA) determine that some material may not be suitable for preteenagers' viewing, while other material is not suitable for anyone under age seventeen to witness. Any decision made by groups such as these is strongly driven by their values.

Many groups are defined by and exist because of their values. Their participants are together because they have a common concern or interest. For example, members of the Parents and Friends of Lesbians and Gays (PFLAG) are all interested in understanding and accepting homosexual children and loved ones because they believe everyone deserves love, respect, and dignity. Other groups develop their values as they continue to interact together. If you were asked to participate on a local Teenage Pregnancy Task Force, you would surely know that everyone on that task force values the idea of "preventing kids from having kids." To find out how this value is applied to specific cases or problems, your task force would need to obtain additional values clarification.

In summary, groups make decisions that are harmonious with their values. By the same token, the processes that groups engage in while making decisions are also value-driven. Discussions of any kind are likely to be highly controlled by a group's values. Even though a group may attempt to clarify its values in advance of its meetings, leaders may need to remind the members of these values as work continues on a task.

Goals

Effective groups are those whose members are working "on the same page." That is, all participants in a group envision, support, and devote their efforts to the same result or product. Goals are those results or products. Recall

---

CHECKLIST

Values Clarification

Rank the values in the left-hand column in their order of importance to you as an individual. Then rank the group values in the right-hand column in their order of importance to you as a group member.

Individual Values	Group Values
1. _____ Spiritual fulfillment	1. _____ Consensus building
2. _____ World peace	2. _____ Group productivity
3. _____ Marital bliss	3. _____ Conflict management
4. _____ Honesty	4. _____ Group cohesiveness
5. _____ Career achievement	5. _____ Cordial relations among members
6. _____ Secure financial situation	6. _____ Popularity among group members
7. _____ Professional recognition	7. _____ Group recognition

Look at your rankings. Do you find that there are similarities in your personal values and your group values?

our earlier discussion about the five steps you should follow in formulating and setting effective goals (see the checklist "A Group Leader's Strategies for Effective Goal Setting"). That information is relevant to this discussion.

A group's failure to clarify its goals before beginning work on a project can prove disastrous. Here is a classic example of a group that was not goal-directed. Several years ago, a university professor was working on an awards task force for a professional organization. All anyone knew about the task force was that it had been formed to make nominations and recommendations to the association's board of directors regarding individuals who should receive awards. Prior to the group's first meeting, no attempt was made to define any of the following: the kind of awards to be given, the number of people to be nominated for each award, the criteria for an award nominee, or even the date when the nominations had to be submitted for board approval. When the task force convened at the association's annual convention just two days before the award winners were to be announced, there was total chaos. After almost two hours of fruitless discussion, someone finally retrieved a copy of the association's bylaws and discovered that it contained exact titles for the awards and specific criteria for each.

Many people confuse group goals with objectives and use these two terms interchangeably. Goals are the end-states or products that a group aspires to achieve, whereas objectives are the specific and measurable means that lead to the goals. A series of objectives usually relate to a single goal. For example, a hospital acquisitions task force has a goal of purchasing the newest X-ray equipment for all of its examination rooms by the end of the year. This group may have several objectives that lead to that goal: (1) to have six major community corporations make donations of $5,000 by June; (2) to persuade 65 percent of all employees to donate $1 from each paycheck for six months; (3) to make a 45 percent down payment on the equipment by September 1; and (4) to place six articles describing the project in community publications by March 3.

MANAGING GROUP EXPECTATIONS

Several factors determine whether a group's meeting is successful or unsuccessful. Without doubt, the expectations and goals that participants bring with them to a meeting play a major role. You are already well aware of the importance of expectations in communication. Green and Lazarus conducted a survey of over 1,000 business leaders, which revealed several of the expectations held by group members and leaders:[9]

- Approximately 85 percent of the respondents expected to spend as much or more time as they currently spend in meetings five years hence.

- One-third of the time spent in meetings is unproductive; therefore, although the time spent in meetings is increasing, time wasted is also growing, with an estimated loss to business in excess of $40 billion.

- Ninety-seven percent of respondents believed that participants should be prepared for meetings, but only 28 percent were prepared most of the time.
- Three out of four meetings fail to end on schedule.
- Two out of three meetings fail to achieve their goals.

The many reasons for these opinions and observations are linked to individual expectations, which are so often violated, thus causing dissatisfaction with group processes.

DEALING WITH TIME PRESSURES IN GROUPS

The amount of time a group has available can play a significant role in the way it makes decisions. **Time pressures**—the effects of a shortage of time on the decision-making process—can influence two aspects of group decision making: planning and leadership styles.

Planning to Avoid Time Pressures

Planning and coordinating are essential activities for effective decision making. You probably know people who would "build a bridge" before they knew what river or lake it was going to cover! Similarly, groups can make decisions without engaging in proper planning and coordinating activities. Although a group might have a variety of reasons to proceed without planning and coordinating, time pressures are usually the major reason why a group fails to do so.

Consider this example. A group from a professional corporation was working on team-building processes in an outdoor simulation. The group started the activity with its twelve members standing on a wooden platform. They had one long and one short wooden plank at their disposal to assist in moving to a second platform and then to a third. Neither the participants nor the wooden planks could touch the ground; if they did so, the group would have to start over.

The simulation had two trials. In the first trial, the group was given only five minutes to complete the task. In the second, the group had unlimited time. Not surprisingly, very little advance planning or coordinating was possible in the first trial. The group member with the loudest voice prevailed and announced the "plan" for the group to follow. The group did so, and it failed miserably. In the second trial, with plenty of time available, the group mapped out an elaborate strategy by which to complete the simulation. The participants debated and questioned each other, reevaluated ideas, and then finally reached a consensus agreement on how to proceed. The group completed the simulation successfully in only twelve minutes.

Using Leadership Styles to Avoid Time Pressures

The style a group leader uses is also dependent on time. Remember the four different styles discussed earlier, each of which varies in the degree to which the leader allows group members to be involved in decision making. There are many reasons why group leaders may choose not to involve subordinates in decision making. For example, subordinates do not possess the knowledge or experience needed to assist in making the decision, or the subordinates do not want to participate. Yet of all the possible examples, time pressures appear to be the most important.

Many leaders who believe in participative techniques are often forced to be authoritarian leaders simply because there is no time for the group to participate in making a particular decision. In crisis situations, participative techniques may indeed yield a better decision, but time will not permit them. Consider the example of a military unit in the field of battle, with grenades and enemy fire exploding around it. There is no time for the leader to say, "What do you think we should do?" The leader must say, "Get your butt down in the ditch and don't move until I order you to!"

On the other hand, groups need not always be at the mercy of time, even in the face of strong pressures. Here are three ways that groups can work around time and produce a quality decision:

- **A group may begin a discussion by taking a nonbinding poll.** Suppose a city council is discussing whether to join a regional mass transit association. The decision must be made by the end of the meeting. The leader may begin by asking how many of the members favor the union and how many are opposed to it. A straw poll will save a group time; the group will not have to discuss items on which all participants already agree. In addition, this vote gives the group an idea of how far apart the participants are on a topic.

- **The leader may impose time limits on certain components of a discussion.** For example, one rule might be that no one speaker may have the floor for more than five minutes. Another might be that once a person has spoken on a topic, that person cannot contribute to the group without specific permission from the leader. Yet another might be that open discussion will take place for sixty minutes. At that time, the group will take a vote.

- **The group may not make any decision at all.** No decision is often better than a bad decision. As Covey argues, "No deal basically means that if we can't find a solution that would benefit us both, we agree to disagree agreeably—No Deal. No expectations have been created, no performance contracts established."[10] Why make a bad decision that you will regret later because time pressures have forced you into it? Stop, table the discussion, or postpone reaching a conclusion.

WORKING THROUGH CONFLICT

The best decisions are usually those that have followed productive conflict. This means that clarification questions are asked, participants' ideas are challenged, counter-examples are presented, "worst-case" scenarios are considered, and proposals are reformulated. After such a process, a group can have confidence that its decision has been tested. If an idea survives these rigorous tests, it has a fighting chance to be successful when it is actually applied.

The other advantage of conflict is that group members will "own" the decision that is reached. Because they have had a part in analyzing, synthesizing, and constructing the decision, and because they have participated in its "shakedown," group members will generally agree with, adhere to, and defend the decision before others.

This explains why people prefer consensus decision making to majority vote. When a group takes a split-decision vote, at least one person will be dissatisfied and believe that the decision was forced. Conversely, when the participants argue about the decision and have had a chance to question and test a proposal, they will have had their "ten cents' worth" put on the table and will own part of the resulting decision. Unfortunately, time constraints may prevent a group from using the consensus method. However, it should be employed whenever possible.

THE PROCESS OF DECISION MAKING IN GROUPS AND TEAMS

Effective groups do not make decisions arbitrarily or haphazardly.[11] Rather, they engage in very systematic processes that result in consensus decisions that all participants can understand and to which they can commit themselves. Here is an eight-step process that has worked for many groups (see Figure 3.1). For clarity, one example is used throughout this section. Pretend that you are a member of a neighborhood group that is meeting to reduce crime in the area.

IDENTIFY THE PROBLEM

As a first step, a group must make sure that all its members are in agreement on the main problem to be solved. If the group's goal is to generate a solution, then all of its members really must understand the problem in the same way.

This step does not mean that the group simply announces the problem, then agrees on it and moves on. Thus, in the example, the simple statement "We need to find a way to reduce crime in our neighborhood" would not be enough. Instead, this step involves gaining a thorough understanding of the problem the group is addressing.

The group should begin by having each participant share his or her perception of the problem. No debate or questions should be allowed until all members have had a chance to voice their perceptions. In this way, the leader will have an idea of how far apart the members are in their thinking about the

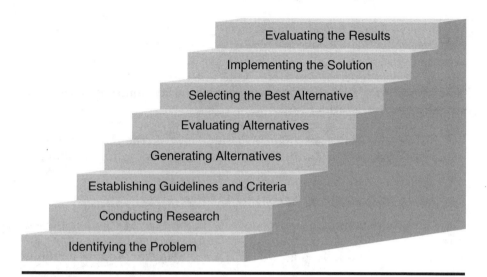

FIGURE 3.1 The decision-making process.

problem. For example, one member might say, "We have inadequate street lighting," while another might suggest, "We do very little looking out for each other."

Next, the group should engage in an extensive analysis of the problem. The members should question each other, debate ideas, and attempt to clarify positions. They should provide philosophies, statistics, case examples, incidents, or analogies in making their analysis. During this step, the group asks questions such as, What are the origins or causes of this problem? What are the possible ramifications if the problem is not solved? What is the philosophy behind the current state of affairs? Who is affected? To what extent?

Before moving on, the leader should make sure all the participants agree on the problem. The leader should also summarize the discussion that has been held up to that point. If the members have not reached agreement, the leader should pinpoint the source of confusion and proceed to obtain a consensus.

CONDUCT RESEARCH

After the group has agreed on the exact problem to be solved, more information may be needed in some areas. Research may be required to:

- bridge gaps in information so that the problem can be analyzed properly
- obtain clarification in order to resolve two or more inconsistent views expressed by participants
- review the historical success of a proposed solution

In the neighborhood example, the group may not know the exact number of burglaries or the approximate dollar figures lost because of crime in the area. Some participants may want to know the actual cost of installing motion detectors on each person's property. Others may oppose that view and propose investigating the cost of hiring a private security company to patrol the neighborhood on a regular basis.

Without conducting research on these and other topics, the group operates out of ignorance or misperception. As a rule, better decisions are made when group members are armed with data and facts rather than with speculation.

ESTABLISH GUIDELINES AND CRITERIA

Once the group thoroughly understands the problem and has done sufficient research on it, the participants should discuss the criteria by which any solution they propose will be judged. This is not the time to propose solutions; that comes later.

In this step, the group agrees on the guidelines to be used to evaluate solutions. In the neighborhood crime example, the criteria may be requirements such as (1) a cost of under $500 per family, (2) the involvement of all families in the neighborhood, and (3) adherence to the guidelines of the city housing code.

As in step 1, group members should question each other to obtain more information or clarification. The group's goal is to reach consensus on the criteria. Although several criteria may be selected, they must be independent of each other. Before proceeding, the leader should again verify that all members agree on the criteria they will use to judge the solutions. In the event of disagreements or problems, the leader should identify the point of confusion and reopen the discussion. In order to be able to use these criteria later, the leader should record each of them on a flip-chart or blackboard.

GENERATE ALTERNATIVES

Unlike the previous steps, this step is actually just brainstorming. Each group member should contribute as many desirable solutions as possible, and the leader should record them as they are expressed.

This step is not interactive; that is, the group members do not now debate the worth of the proposed solutions. Each step is simply stated and recorded by the leader.

In the neighborhood crime example, you may hear proposals such as:

- Install professional security equipment in each home, and negotiate the purchase with group buying power.
- Close off two access roads after 11:00 P.M.
- Have four to six residents patrol the area on foot in pairs each evening.

- Encourage each family to buy a guard dog.
- Offer to house-sit for families who are out of town for extended periods of time.

EVALUATE ALTERNATIVES

In this step, the group weighs each solution provided in the previous step against the criteria the members have agreed on. It is essential at this point that the group use as much high-quality information as possible, so that it can adequately consider the positive and negative qualities of the proposed alternatives. Groups must be careful to weigh all evidence for all alternatives to ensure that the decisions eventually reached can be supported with good solid arguments.[12]

The leader can then announce the first proposed solution and ask the group whether the solution meets criterion number 1 and, if so, criterion number 2, and so forth, until the solution either meets all the criteria or is eliminated. This process should be continued until all of the solutions have been examined.

In the case of the neighborhood crime example, the leader may say, "Okay, let's look at the first proposal—that we install professional security equipment in each home and negotiate the price with our group buying power. Now, does that mesh well with our first criterion—that it cost under $500 per family?"

SELECT THE BEST ALTERNATIVE

Once the group has arrived at a short list of alternatives, the members must select one alternative that can best fill their needs. Groups that are lucky may indeed find the perfect solution. That is, only one proposed solution successfully survives the evaluation. Frequently, however, one of two other things happens. Either more than one solution survives, or no solution survives. What should you do? In the first case, the group should determine whether the two or more viable solutions are mutually exclusive. Can you do both of them? If so, there is no problem, for you have two (or more) solutions that you can implement immediately. If not, pick the solution that has met the criteria most completely. This is likely to be your best solution.

In the event that no solution survives, the group must choose at least one of the previously suggested solutions—that is, the proposed solution that meets the greatest number of criteria. Although that solution may not be optimal, it is superior to any of the others.

By following this example, you can probably see that the step that establishes criteria is just as important as—if not more important than—the step that produces solutions. If the criteria are worthwhile standards, the group can feel comfortable with its solution.

IMPLEMENT THE SOLUTION

The last two steps in the decision-making process are implementing and then evaluating the solution reached by the group. Implementing a solution involves putting into action the ideas and decisions that the group has finalized. In some cases, this means submitting a report to a higher authority, with recommendations about how the solution can best be activated. For example, a self-directed work team in business will go through the decision-making process to arrive at a recommendation for improving some aspect of the organization. The team's recommendation is then forwarded to an executive committee, a task force, or an individual responsible for seeing that the solution is implemented in the organization.

In other cases, the group suggesting the solution is also expected to implement it. In order to do so, the group is usually expected to convert general or abstract ideas into a practical plan of action. Because most group decisions affect more people than just the group members, directions and instructions for carrying out the decision must be clear, direct, and simple. In addition, many people will want to know the reasons why a particular decision was reached. Therefore, your action plan should include some explanation of your decision and a justification for implementing it in the way you propose.

EVALUATE THE RESULTS

Solutions resulting from the group decision-making process must stand the test of evaluation. Solutions are best evaluated by returning to the criteria that were established early in the process. The following questions can be helpful as you apply the group's criteria to your solution.

- Were the criteria useful and appropriate for the problem?
- How strictly were the criteria used in arriving at the solution?
- What other criteria would have been helpful in reaching a better solution?
- Does the solution have any weaknesses or disadvantages?

Evaluating a group decision can make a good decision even better. A hard look at any result or outcome will uncover even minor shortcomings that can be eliminated before full implementation takes place. Careful scrutiny can create opportunities for precision. In addition, evaluation can help groups to improve their decision making in the future. Learning from mistakes is rarely pleasant at the time, but it can help you prevent similar problems in subsequent group work.

The steps involved in the decision-making process are a proven method of producing competent group outcomes. The sequence of steps encourages group members to think reflectively about their task. In this way, all relevant facts and opinions can be discussed and evaluated, thereby ensuring a better decision. You can also use this process for making individual decisions in your personal and professional life.

EVALUATING THE DECISION-MAKING COMPETENCE OF GROUPS AND TEAMS

Groups that plan to be together and meet on a regular, consistent basis should plan to evaluate their performance periodically. Without assessing where the group stands in terms of its goals, how well the group works together, or what kind of problems exist, a group will not reach its full potential.

Groups may be likened to automobiles. If either a car or a group is to run smoothly, its performance must be assessed and its components maintained. **Group evaluations** are a measure of how effectively a group performs as a whole. This section discusses various methods for assessing and evaluating groups.

Numerous categories, rating forms, and questionnaires have been designed to assess the strength of groups. These evaluations usually assess both groups and their individual members.

GROUP EVALUATIONS

Kowitz and Knutson have done outstanding work on evaluating groups as a whole.[13] They divide their scheme into three dimensions for group evaluation:

- informational
- procedural
- interpersonal

Informational Dimensions of Group Evaluation

Informational dimensions are concerned with the group's designated task. According to Kowitz and Knutson, several areas may be assessed. One deals with whether or not the group is working on a task that requires interaction. If the task does not require discussion and does not need the participation of group members with diverse backgrounds and experience, or work on specialized tasks by particular people, the topic needs expansion. Alternatively, perhaps the group should drop the topic or have only one or two individuals address it.

If the task is suitable, is the group prepared for discussion? How much of the necessary research or planning is accomplished prior to the meeting? Does the group recognize the need to get more information before making a decision?

Does the group analyze the problem well? If so, is it creative? What is the quality of information giving, opinion giving, evaluation and criticism, elaboration, and integration among the group's members?

Procedural Dimensions of Group Evaluation

The procedural functions of a group refer to the ways in which the group coordinates its activities and communication. The key functions to be evaluated include eliciting communication, delegating and directing action, summarizing group activity, conflict management, process evaluation, and tension release. You might see a few problems regarding these areas.

One problem frequently associated with groups is the tendency of some members to talk too much while others give too little input. This problem requires a leader or other members to employ gatekeeping, which is an attempt to keep the lines of communication open among all group members. A leader may interrupt with a line such as, "Harry, I think we should hear from some other people on this subject."

Another problem occurs when issues that have already been decided on surface for a second time. When this happens, many members express frustration with the process. Someone may say, "These are the craziest meetings," or "This is a big waste of my time." A leader or another member can use one of two options in this situation. One option is to use summarizing. Summarizing contributions sound like "What we've been talking about is . . ." or "So, what we seem to be saying is . . ." A second option is to steer the group back toward its objectives. The question becomes: What is the group trying to accomplish, and how is the discussion at this moment helping to accomplish those objectives?

Finally, members may need to release tension at certain points during a meeting. They can do so by telling a joke or an anecdote, by letting members tell each other how they feel at a given moment, and the like. Clearly, participants may lose sight of their individual responsibilities and importance in the overall group context. Once members are reminded of what is expected of them, tension can decrease and the group can resume making progress.

Interpersonal Dimensions of Group Evaluation

In this part of the evaluation, the assessment focuses on the relationships that exist among the members while the task is being accomplished. If these relationships are strained, uncomfortable, or unpleasant, the productivity and results will be affected in negative ways. Four topics can be assessed here: positive reinforcement, solidarity, cooperativeness, and respect toward others.

As already noted, one of the most dangerous points in a meeting is reached when conflict shifts from tasks to personalities. Expressions such as "When you've been around here as long as I have, you can talk to me about it" do nothing to advance the group's work.

INDIVIDUAL EVALUATIONS

Apart from examining the group as a whole, each individual participant may be evaluated. An **individual evaluation** determines how well members help the group accomplish its task and how well they perform their functions in the process. Samovar and King have created an excellent scheme for evaluating individual members as well as leaders.[14] The components that can be evaluated are as follows.

Each of the following eleven topics can be used to assess group participants:

- preparation
- speaking
- listening
- open-mindedness
- sensitivity to others
- value of information
- value of thinking
- group orientation
- value of procedural contributions
- assistance in leadership function
- overall evaluation

There are eleven other topics that can be used to assess a definite or designated leader:

- opening the discussion
- asking appropriate questions
- offering reviews
- clarifying ideas
- encouraging critical evaluation
- limiting irrelevancies
- protecting minority viewpoints
- remaining impartial
- keeping accurate records
- concluding discussion
- exerting overall leadership

4 Communicating in Organizations

THE NEED FOR EFFECTIVE COMMUNICATION IN ORGANIZATIONS

Organizations are everywhere. Perhaps you belong to religious organizations, political organizations, civic organizations, fraternal organizations, and/or business organizations. Organizations exist in order to bring people together for a common purpose so that their combined energies can be channeled into a greater good. The only way that organizations can succeed, or even exist for that matter, is through communication. Often referred to as **organizational communication**, this process involves the exchange of messages between organizational members or among members of different organizations. You will find instances of information processing, interpersonal communication, small group communication, and public speaking in most organizations. However, when these types of communication occur within a certain organizational context, different norms and rules apply than if the same communication occurred in a different context. Being an effective communicator requires that you take into consideration the organizational context.

As you learn about various aspects of organizational communication, you improve your chances of success. It is important for you to know about the culture of an organization and how it is structured because these aspects affect how you create and send messages. You will also become familiar with several of the most prevalent contexts in organizations, such as superior-subordinate relationships, interdepartmental relationships, and interorganizational relationships. In addition, you will learn how to use basic communication skills in the organization, including team building, networking, negotiating, and using channels and technology for greater success.

HOW DOES ORGANIZATIONAL COMMUNICATION DIFFER FROM OTHER TYPES OF COMMUNICATION?

Becoming a competent communicator in the organizational setting requires that you understand how other people in this context send messages. Depending on the size of the organization, literally hundreds of messages are sent and received in any given day. The messages that you send could be lost, ignored, or neglected if you do not have a sense of how the overall organization communicates. Therefore, seeing the big picture is essential for commu-

GROUP COMMUNICATION IN CULTURAL PERSPECTIVE

Cultural Diversity in the Workforce

Consider the following example of cultural diversity in the workplace. Universal Industries is a supplier of light electronic equipment in a large city in the southwest. Leeva Wao, a forty-two-year-old Japanese woman, serves as director of personnel. Leeva's employees include managers Henry Tento, a forty-four-year-old white male who has been with Universal for twenty years; Mena Galon, a young Latino woman who was promoted at Universal last year; and George Allen, an African American male who came to Universal from a competitor. Leeva's assistant is Luana Battinni, an Italian woman of thirty-nine. Luana uses a motorized wheelchair due to a degenerative nerve disease. The department also has a coordinator of benefits whose name is Yang Lin, a sixty-two-year-old woman who emigrated from China in the late 1970s.

The diversity of Universal's personnel department is typical of today's workforce. Consequently, intercultural communication is a major issue within business organizations. Recall from earlier chapters some of the problems and benefits of intercultural communication. What barriers to communication (e.g., ethnocentrism, stereotyping) might arise among the employees in Universal's personnel department? How might Leeva Wao, as the director, help to break down these barriers? Will the employees from low-context cultures have problems communicating with their co-workers from high-context cultures? Why? What are some benefits of a multicultural personnel department, both for Universal Industries and for the individual employees?

nication success. Two important viewpoints provide this type of understanding. In the following sections, you learn how the culture of the organization affects communication and how applying systems theory to your organization facilitates effective communication.

ORGANIZATIONAL CULTURE

Organizational culture—its members' relatively stable perceptions of their organization and its norms—emerges over time, in much the same way as the cultures of nations or ethnic groups develop.[1] As you know, competent communication requires you to understand both the culture and the context in which you are communicating. As with other types of cultures, an organizational culture provides guidance about appropriate norms and behaviors.

In any organization, certain communication behaviors are either encouraged or discouraged. For example, some organizations develop an open culture, in which people are encouraged to question things and suggest change. Other organizations discourage communication and do not elicit new ideas. Some individuals may feel more comfortable in "closed" organizations; they come to work, do their individual jobs, and then return to their own personal lives. Other people prefer family type organizations, in which personal and work life are closely tied together.[2] (The characteristic of openness is discussed again in the next section.)

An organization usually develops customs and rituals that contribute to its organizational culture. For example, employee award ceremonies may reinforce the values of hard work and creativity. In many companies, "dress-down Friday" allows the suit-and-tie crowd to be more casual and is often accompanied by more in-house communication, including joking and teasing. Other organizations, however, would never allow a dress-down day; their customs include a commitment to formal dress — and probably clear boundaries on many other types of communication.

Organizational culture also includes the degree to which an organization tolerates risk. Some companies reward the employee who goes out on a limb to test a new idea; others are conservative, preferring clear guidelines and policies to govern their members. An organization's tolerance for conflict is another indication of its culture. Some organizations see conflict as healthy and as part of a growth process, while others try to avoid conflict at all costs and at all levels of the organization.

Although an organizational culture develops over time, once it is formed it remains fairly constant. New members are usually assimilated into the culture, learning its values, goals, customs, and behaviors. In some organizations, however, subcultures develop, with clear — and different — views of their own. Subcultures may contest the views of the organizational culture by not cooperating with policies and procedures, not consulting with authorities, and not participating in the customs of the organization. Obviously, such actions cause conflict and division in the organization.[3] Some experts argue that certainty about an organizational culture is unlikely in today's society and that constant communication is necessary if an organization is to be effective.

They believe that there is a greater tolerance for diversity in modern organizations and that their constant communication efforts are actually a reflection of their significant commitment to tolerate differences.[4]

Within an organizational culture, then, many communication challenges exist. Organizations involved in international business have even more challenges. Not only do they try to improve communication within their own organization, but they are likely to have to accommodate both national cultures and many different organizational cultures.

ORGANIZATIONAL SYSTEMS

Understanding how communication actually works in organizations is not an easy process, but viewing organizations as systems is helpful. When you study biological systems (plants, animals, etc.) you come to understand how particular plants or animals exist within larger systems and how they are affected by the environment (food, water, temperature) and other organisms. Organizations as systems are similar; they are seldom closed, that is, completely independent. Modern organizations must interact with the economy and with politics at national as well as international levels. Even small local changes may affect the organization in profound ways.

A **system** is a unique whole that consists of the members who have relationships with one another in a particular environment.[5] In organizations, this means that no person can work in isolation, that no company can insulate itself from the interactions of its members, and that outside forces can change the communication processes of organizations. Consider the example of a college or university system—a system you are surely familiar with. Some of its members are faculty, students, office staff, financial aid personnel, and the bursar, all of whom have relationships with one another. The college exists within its environment, which includes other systems that have a direct impact on it. These other systems in our example are the city and state where the college is located; the legislature, which affects tuition; part-time employers for students and positions for graduates; families who support students; and high schools that supply students. What other systems affect the college or university you attend?

There is more to systems than just members, relationships, and the environment. In order to understand organizations as systems, it is important to learn about their underlying qualities or characteristics. These include wholeness, interdependence, hierarchy, openness, adaptability, and equifinality.[6]

Wholeness is a characteristic that refers to a system's unique configuration. Thus, an organization is not just a collection of departments or individuals; these entities fit together in a way that makes the organization special. An organization can also be adjusted, realigned, or reconfigured and still maintain its wholeness. Departmental reorganizations or administrative shifts, for example, do not threaten the wholeness of an organization. Suppose that you work at a place we'll call Best Bank. The bank has several departments, such as loan processing, accounting, auditing, new accounts, and public relations, which collectively make up the organization. If the bank decides to separate the new accounts department into "checking accounts" and "savings accounts," the wholeness of the organization will still be intact.

As you may recall from earlier discussions, interdependence is an important characteristic affecting group communication. Interdependence is just as important in a system. In a business organization, any hiring, firing, loss, or acquisition affects the entire system. For instance, the change in the new accounts department at Best Bank would cause changes in other departments: Auditing might set up a new bookkeeping system; administration may hire new employees; and the public relations department might devise a new advertising campaign to announce the change.

Reflecting the natural order of organisms in the world, organizations have hierarchies. A **hierarchy** is the classification of a group of people according to ability, status, function, or other criteria. Thus, individuals in a system can be identified as being related to other individuals that are above them, below them, or on the same level of hierarchy as they are. At Best Bank, for example, new account representatives work together in their department and are all on the same level of hierarchy. They report to the vice president in charge of accounts, who is above them in the organization's hierarchy.

Another important characteristic of systems is **openness**. In order to avoid becoming a "closed" system, in which the organization will collapse in on itself, a system must maintain openness by correcting any imbalances. The organization does this by using feedback to identify areas of imbalance and correcting tendencies to "topple." For example, for many years the railroad industry was a closed system. Few new ideas flowed into the organization. Members defined themselves as being in the "railroad business," perceiving themselves to be the only game in town. When other means of transporting people and goods in a less costly and more efficient manner became available (trucks, airlines, etc.), the railroad industry went bankrupt. However, once railroad companies opened up their system to new ideas and designed new ways of generating business, their members began to redefine themselves as being in the "transportation business."

The Chrysler Corporation is another example of a failed closed system. Initially, Chrysler manufactured only large luxury cars. They were a closed system intent on doing the same thing they always did — making large cars. When gasoline prices increased to $1.00 a gallon, they still refused to make smaller, more fuel-efficient cars. Consumers began to look elsewhere to find cars that drank less gas. As a result, Chrysler went bankrupt. The "new" Chrysler Corporation is much more open to consumer needs and is a very successful open system.

The modern organization is a dynamic, changing system. In fact, change is probably the only constant of organizations. For this reason, **adaptability** is an indispensable quality; it enables a system to adjust to changes in politics, economics, individuals, or ideas. Best Bank may have divided its new accounts department because the local economy improved, producing an increase in savings accounts. Or it may have reorganized because its customers wanted two divisions, or because an employee suggested it as a more efficient way to handle accounts. Whatever the reason, Best Bank was adaptable enough to make the change.

The final goals, or end-states, of an organization may be accomplished in any number of ways. In other words, a system is capable of generating multiple ideas and multiple behaviors for attaining its results. This characteristic is known as **equifinality**. Let's look at our example again. Best Bank is responsible for producing a profit and ensuring the security of depositors' funds. The loan processing department provides loans, the collections department receives loan payments, tellers take deposits and cash checks. Although these are multiple behaviors and are accomplished in a variety of ways, they all contribute to the final goals of the organization.

ORGANIZATIONAL RELATIONSHIPS

We have discussed the idea that the organizational culture provides guidance for appropriate communicative behavior. So, also, does the context of an interaction. Within an organization, communication is evaluated in terms of the relationships that develop at the workplace. As you know from earlier chapters, in order to become a competent communicator, you need to consider the relational contexts of your interactions. The following sections describe some of the different communication contexts that exist in organizations.

Relationships between Superiors and Subordinates

Communication between managers and employees still constitutes most of the work-related conversation in organizations. Even though teams are now commonplace, thus increasing the amount of employee-to-employee communication, the boss and employee still must communicate about many issues, such as the status of tasks or projects, grievances, morale, influences from other departments on a department's work, and annual performance reviews.

Relationships between Team Leaders and Team Members

Over the past years, organizations have changed from the "skilled leader" approach (Theory X) to the "skilled people" approach (Theory Y)[7] to the team management approach, known as **Theory Z.**[8] This approach requires that both the manager and the other members of the organizational group participate in management decision making—that they build teams together.

Building teams involves many of the small group communication skills we discussed earlier. An effective manager will build an energetic work group that produces high-quality results. The group members will enjoy both their common goals and the interaction among themselves. In short, an effective team builds strong relationships while still getting the work done.

An effective manager will determine when and if team building needs to occur.[9] If a group's function can be performed better individually, if there is a history of poor relationships that would make team building difficult, or if the larger organization does not support such an approach, the manager may decide against team building.

But teams consistently outperform individuals in organizations today, so the effective manager is often a good team leader. This team leader acts as a coach, providing the vision for the team, giving it structure and organization, and helping it to remain focused. The effective coach links team efforts to those of the overall organization, so that team members understand the

CHECKLIST

Strategies for Superiors and Subordinates

Interestingly, the setting, or context, in which a manager meets with an employee is critical to the communication process, the satisfaction of both participants, and the results. You are well aware of the fact that a manager and employee bring expectations and goals to a meeting and that these affect what will be said during the course of the meeting. If a manager wants to ensure that a meeting with an employee has every chance to succeed, he or she should follow these guidelines.

✓ Schedule adequate time for the meeting.

✓ Minimize distractions or interruptions, including phone calls or visitors.

✓ Approach the meeting with an open mind and communicate that to the employee by asking more questions and making fewer demands.

✓ Communicate sincerity about your desire to meet with the employee.

✓ Exhibit active listening skills, including nonverbal behaviors such as nodding, postural shifts, and appropriate facial expressions.

If you are the subordinate in this dyadic relationship, you can also use your communication skills to influence a positive outcome.

✓ Ask for a meeting time or place that will allow you to achieve your goals.

✓ Clarify your goals and your performance in your own mind before the meeting, so that you can represent yourself adequately to your supervisor.

✓ Make reasonable requests for training, advice, or resources that will enhance your performance or satisfaction.

✓ Exhibit active listening skills (verbal and nonverbal) to communicate your understanding of information or suggestions for improvement.

✓ State your commitment to the department or the organization.

importance of their work within the organizational structure. The effective coach also enhances the relationships of the team members, facilitating the development of trust and supportiveness. Finally, the effective coach helps others on the team develop leadership skills themselves, thus enhancing their confidence and productivity.

When a group works exceptionally well together, it may become a self-managing team. In such a case, the manager becomes the coach "on the sidelines," providing supporting ideas and comments for the team. Regardless of the manager's particular role on the team, the effective manager needs small group communication skills to build a highly effective, productive group.

Relationships between Organizational Departments

Cooperation between departments is a must in modern organizations. Marketing departments must work with the sales force in order to produce proper advertising materials for the marketplace. Office services must store and obtain sufficient computer supplies so that other departments can generate documents, correspondence, manuals, and so forth. Personnel departments must recruit the best candidates for job openings so that work in other departments may be performed properly. A company's mail room is also critical to its success. If documents and correspondence are not distributed properly and efficiently, employees may not be able to do their jobs.

Within an organization, the greatest communication issues often involve negotiating responsibility between two departments. Which department oversees what function? Which department head has the final say for approval? Is it appropriate to cross traditional departmental lines in order to accomplish work? Departments need adequate answers to such questions if they are to function effectively within the larger system.

Let us now look at the relationships between organizations. An organization uses many other organizations to conduct business. These include printers, couriers, electrical technicians, advertising agencies, groundskeepers, software developers, travel agencies, and training consultants. With today's emphasis on quality and customer service, many organizations know that in order to make money, they must take an increasing interest in the work and prosperity of the companies they serve. To accomplish this, frequent and accurate communication between organizations is essential.

No longer is it adequate for companies to offer only the "lowest price" or the "best service." They also must compete for long-term relationships with their customers who are always interested in doing business more efficiently. Communicating honest expectations and providing candid feedback are two of the most important skills in fostering these relationships. In many cases, the partnerships that organizations form between themselves make it difficult to determine which one is in fact the customer. Not too long ago, in a stunning role reversal, two advertising agencies actually fired organizations that were their clients because they no longer wished to represent those companies!

DEVELOPING EFFECTIVE SKILLS IN ORGANIZATIONAL COMMUNICATION

As we have seen, there are various channels through which to communicate. In organizations, these channels may involve many people who are superior or subordinate to you in rank and position. Thus, understanding how to handle these channels is very important. In the section that follows, you learn how to master several communication skills that are critical for your professional success.

USE COMMUNICATION CHANNELS

You already know that a channel is a vehicle or mechanism for transmitting messages. In organizations, there are many such vehicles, including telephones, memos, letters, e-mail transmissions, and face-to-face conversations. We can also speak of two broad types of organizational channels: formal and informal.

Formal channels are the communication paths established along the hierarchical lines of an organization. These paths typically come from the organizational chart of the company and involve such issues as status, authority, and power (see Figure 4.1). For example, many companies would consider a funding request memo from a sales representative to a regional vice president quite inappropriate unless the request had first received approval from a mid-level division or district sales manager. Formal communication channels also would not allow a chief executive officer to receive suggestions from entry-level employees unless the messages had first been screened by mid- and upper-level managers. As you might suspect, when you use formal communication channels, you should use formal communication methods. Thus, you would use written documentation, such as memos and letters, much more often than face-to-face conversation. In some companies, when employees write a formal memo or letter, both the sender's boss and the recipient's immediate boss must receive a copy.

Informal channels refer to the "grapevine" as well as to unauthorized communication between two or more persons in an organization (see Figure 4.2). The grapevine is another term for "rumor mill," which is an ambiguous

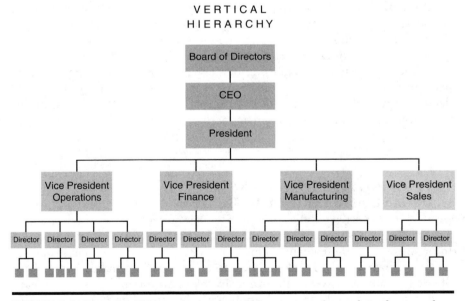

VERTICAL
HIERARCHY

FIGURE 4.1 A vertical hierarchy such as this one requires a lot of upward and downward communication along formal channels.

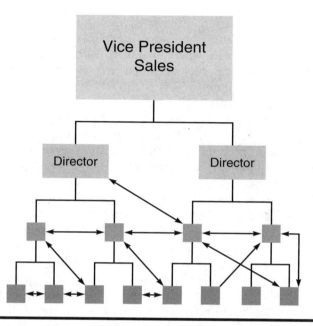

FIGURE 4.2 Informal channels allow messages to move across departments and hierarchical lines.

but accurate description in most organizations. Frequently, large numbers of employees are aware of personnel, policy, or procedural changes long before they ever appear in a memo or are announced at a meeting. Even when policies and formal lines of communication are supposed to prevent the transmission of information, those individuals who have friendships with key communicators frequently "leak" even the most confidential of information.

The key to using communication channels properly in an organization is to know what is expected. What are the norms for the organization? If formality is the rule, be clear and succinct. Be sure that the right people receive copies of your correspondence and other documents. If informality is the rule, be visible. Become known, increase your popularity, get out of your office, and get to know other people. Hang around the break room when you know key employees will be there. Stay on top of who is promoted to what job, who works for whom, and who is moving to what position in the company. Know when and where to discuss nonwork topics such as who is getting married, who is dating whom, or what kind of car someone bought. The more you are a resource for others, the more you will be a recipient of informal news as well.

USE COMMUNICATION NETWORKS

As you recall from our earlier discussion, **networks** are the communication patterns used within groups. In other words, networks are "who talks to whom about what" in an organization. The more "connected" an individual is to the participants in an organizational network, the more centralized he or she is. A **centralized network** is one in which a majority of the communication passes through a small number of participants, maybe even just through one person. Conversely, a **decentralized network** is one in which many participants have a number of connections to others. An example of a centralized network would be where employees in a unit interact less among themselves than with their boss, such as outside sales representatives who have most of their organizational communication with the sales manager. An example of a decentralized network would be a fast-food restaurant where employees must interact with several other employees in order to serve food products. The diagrams in Figure 4.3 illustrate the differences between these two types of network.

Research indicates that there are many advantages to being in a centralized position in a network. In general, there seem to be apparent advantages to cultivating frequent and meaningful relationships with others. Centralized persons are more likely to emerge as leaders,[10] report higher satisfaction with their tasks, have higher morale,[11] experience less job tedium and burnout,[12] and hold more favorable perceptions of their organization.[13]

Today, **networking** also refers to communicating with others outside a single organization. Defined as "simply people meeting people and profiting from the connection,"[14] networking refers to activities such as striking up conversations and exchanging business cards during airplane travel, prior to professional meetings, in churches, or in restaurant waiting areas. The key is to have people remember who you are and what services you offer.

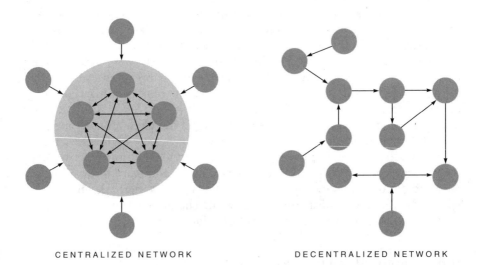

CENTRALIZED NETWORK   DECENTRALIZED NETWORK

FIGURE 4.3 Notice how centralized networks connect more people than do decentralized networks.

Several skills are important for successful networking, whether this is accomplished within or outside of an organization. First, remember and use names. Associate the name with a person or object so that you may recall it easily. Second, be clever about how you describe yourself and what you do. Simply saying "I train sales managers" is not nearly as inviting as "I help companies put money in their pockets." Third, keep an eye out to help others. You never know when someone may return the favor to you. Fourth, try to get a follow-up meeting or conversation scheduled soon. Strike when the iron is hot! To call someone and say "I met you three months ago at a reception" does not pull nearly the same weight as "I spoke with you last night at the party." Fifth, and most important, remember that the time to build network connections is when you need them the least. Join trade associations or non-profit organizations, go to lunch with colleagues outside your department, and attend social functions both inside and outside your typical circle of friends. If you establish these connections in advance, looking for a job or a favor will be much easier than "looking" and "building" at the same time.

NEGOTIATE EFFECTIVELY

Many people think that negotiating only occurs between employees of two organizations, who must meet and mutually agree upon a price, a date, a deadline, a location, a product, or some other factor. While negotiating is involved in all of these examples, negotiating is an internal communication issue as well.

Employees regularly negotiate with their supervisors as well as with each other. Some issues that are commonly negotiated are working hours ("I want to work 9 to 6 instead of 8 to 5 because of my children"); weekend work ("I'll work on Saturday if I can have next Thursday and Friday off"); pay ("You're not worth that much money"); trading-off responsibilities ("I'll do your report if you teach my class"); vacation time ("We'll pay for your hotel room if you switch your vacation days"); or equipment ("I need my own color printer at my desk").

One major issue that many people misunderstand is the role of compromise in negotiating. While compromise is often the outcome of a negotiating session, you should not make it your objective. If your position is realistic and sound, you should argue for it and not back away until you are persuaded to do so. While many negotiators ask for more in the hope of settling for less, we do not recommend this approach. We even know of some cases in which one party set such a lofty, unrealistic goal as an outcome that the other side refused to bargain at all and cut a deal with a different group.

One alternative to compromise, however, is to brainstorm for alternate solutions that please both parties. For example, if you normally work Saturday and Sunday and want the weekend off, you might start out the bargaining session by arguing for a weekend off, validating your position with your work performance and lack of absences. During the negotiations, your supervisor

CHECKLIST

Strategies for Effective Negotiation

Most training programs urge participants to focus on issues and to separate the problem from the person, but the negotiating process is, in fact, usually much more complicated than that. We have found that these five communication behaviors are essential to successful negotiating:

✓ You must listen. You must know and understand the other party's position before you can argue your own successfully.

✓ You must be introspective. One of the fastest ways to shut off bargaining is to speak for your partner instead of speaking for yourself.

✓ You must ask fact-finding questions. Try to uncover the basic who, what, when, where, and why of the other party's position or premise.

✓ You must communicate with an open mind. If you take a defensive, hard-line position, you will close off communication with the other party.

✓ You must keep your emotions in check. Rational negotiating does not need or require anger, hurt feelings, crying, or abrupt withdrawal from the situation.

suggests a compromise and offers you Saturday as a day off. If you compromise, you take Saturday off and work Sunday. If you continue to argue for the whole weekend off, you may be perceived as defensive and inflexible. However, you could suggest alternate solutions that would please both you and your supervisor, such as having a co-worker fill in for you over the weekend, or adding work hours to your other days during the week. Suggesting alternate solutions is often an effective negotiating strategy.

PRACTICE MENTORING

A **mentor** is a member of the organization who is often older, more experienced, and well respected and who serves as a role model for a less-experienced employee (often known as a **protégé**). Mentor-protégé relationships are beneficial to an organization because protégés can develop faster when they learn from someone who has "been there" before. The protégé benefits from this relationship by receiving support, recognition, and friendship from the mentor and through the mentor's influence with other powerful people in the organization. Mentors benefit by demonstrating that they are valuable to the organization and to new employees.

The mentor-protégé relationship depends on a mutual understanding of the roles and characteristics of the people involved. Mentors have knowledge and skills to offer, but protégés must be willing participants. For this relationship to work effectively, a mentor must be approachable, confident, and secure. A protégé must be ambitious, loyal, energetic, and open-minded.

The mentoring relationship will usually progress through four distinct stages:[15]

- **Initiation.** In the initiation stage, the mentor and protégé begin to learn about each other. The mentor shows support by counseling and coaching. The protégé contributes to the relationship by being open to suggestions and by demonstrating loyalty to the mentor.

- **Cultivation.** In the cultivation stage, the mentor and protégé begin to form an interpersonal bond. The mentor begins to protect and promote the protégé, and mutual admiration increases.

- **Separation.** Once a protégé has developed in the organization to a point where the relationship is not as important, the stage of separation usually begins. In this stage, the mentor and protégé drift apart, either physically or emotionally. Several factors can cause separation, but usually one of the members is transferred or promoted, or the protégé becomes increasingly independent of the mentor.

CHECKLIST

Finding a Mentor

If you are working in an organization and want to find an appropriate mentor, the following steps should be useful:

✓ **Ask the personnel or human resources department about formal mentoring programs.** If the organization does not have a formal program, ask your peers about previous mentor-protégé relationships or for the names of possible mentors.

✓ **Identify people on similar career tracks.** People who have followed the same career track that you are on can often serve as excellent mentors.

✓ **Approach a potential mentor and take an interest in what that person does.** Ask questions and demonstrate your enthusiasm to learn. Disclose information about yourself and your interests, and ask him or her for expert advice to improve your productivity.

✓ **Build rapport with someone who you think would be an effective mentor.** Ask if he or she would like to sponsor you in a mentor-protégé relationship. Explain to the person why you think he or she would be a good mentor, and describe your qualifications as a protégé.

SOURCE: K. E. Kram, "Phases of the Mentor Relationship," *Academy of Management Journal* 12 (1983): 608–25.

- **Redefinition.** If the mentoring relationship was successful, the mentor and protégé go through a redefinition of their roles and the relationship. The mentor may still provide advice and expertise, but now both people see the relationship as one of equal partners, where each holds a similar position within the organization.

RESPOND TO SEXUAL HARASSMENT

Although sexual harassment appears to be a recent problem in organizations, it has actually been around a long time.[16] The Equal Employment Opportunity Commission defines **sexual harassment** as unwelcome sexual advances and requests for sexual favors. Sexual harassment is also characterized as verbal or physical conduct of a sexual nature if submission to the conduct is made a condition of employment or if the conduct creates an uncomfortable, intimidating, hostile, or offensive working environment.[17] In other words, sexual harassment is unwelcome and unsolicited behavior of a sexual nature.

Why does sexual harassment occur? Attraction is one reason. One person may become so attracted to another that status and authority are abused in order to obtain sexual satisfaction. A second cause of sexual harassment is power, which can be used to control or dominate the behavior of another. A harasser may think that he or she can wield power over another until sexual favors are delivered.

Communication is another cause of sexual harassment. You have already learned that men and women communicate differently. Females are more likely to self-disclose personal information, and some men might view such disclosures as flirting or sexual advancement. Differences in the sending and receiving of nonverbal cues can also set the stage for sexual harassment. Females often use smiles, eye contact, and touch to indicate interest in a topic or person, whereas men may use these same nonverbal behaviors as openings for sexual intimacy.[18] Some verbal and nonverbal behaviors that indicate sex-

ETHICALLY SPEAKING

Ethics and Sexual Harassment

Defining and identifying sexual harassment can be a problem for organizations and individuals. When do you think behavior is harassment? Is it ethical to report harassment to a supervisor without first confronting the perpetrator? Is it ethical to intervene if you are not directly involved in an incident but only witness it? If your problem concerning sexual harassment were left unresolved by your immediate supervisor, what would you do?

CHECKLIST

Strategies for Addressing Sexual Harassment

Sexual harassment is a degrading and dehumanizing act. You do not have to put up with it. If you think you are being sexually harassed at work, consider the following plan of action:

✓ If you think the behavior of another person is wrong, let that person know. Clearly and firmly tell the harasser that his or her advances are not welcome.

✓ Immediately report the incident to your boss or to someone in the personnel department.

✓ Document each incident in written form; include a description of the incident, the date, the person(s) involved, and any action you took.

✓ If witnesses were present, have them verify the details of the incident.

ual harassment are sexist remarks, embarrassing jokes, taunting, unwelcome remarks, displaying pornographic or offensive materials or photographs, touching affectionately, and kissing.

Sexual harassment often goes unreported because there is a tendency for the victim to avoid confrontation with the perpetrator. In many instances, the victim withdraws from the situation by taking time off from work, transferring to another area, or changing jobs. Often, the victim is reluctant to press charges because the harasser has authority and status.

MASTER COMMUNICATION TECHNOLOGY

In the past twenty years, technology has advanced more rapidly than at any other time in history. These changes in technology are moving organizations in new and exciting directions. In the future, communication technology will allow you, at any time, to send and receive information from anywhere in the world. You will no longer be confined to an office as a place of work. You will use mobile and video phones, choose from five hundred television stations, and use a video screen to read books from libraries around the world.

However, while technology has immeasurable benefits, it presents many challenges for the business communicator. These challenges come from two areas. The first challenge is to understand the rapid advancement and implementation of technologies in your organization. The second challenge is to learn to use the available technology to maximize and enhance your communication skills. This section covers some of the technology tools that will facilitate both oral and written communication.

Pagers

Pagers are simply another article of clothing for many people in business. Estimates indicate that over 31 million people carry pagers. It is quite likely that you will carry some type of pager in the future. Before, a pager was used to emit a beeping sound to alert its user to call a centralized location for a message. Now, pagers beep or vibrate to alert their users that information has been sent. For example, most pagers display telephone numbers and verbal messages that were sent from someone else.

Pagers come in a variety of shapes and sizes. There is a fountain-pen shaped unit that fits neatly in a shirt pocket and a pager in the form of a wristwatch. Some pagers hold dozens of messages; store business information like the Dow Jones industrial average; and save critical information, like the most recent weather report and winning lottery numbers.[18] Voice pagers and pagers the size of credit cards that fit into personal computers (and act like cellular modems) are coming on the market.

CHECKLIST

Tips for Communicating via Telephone

Since you have probably been using a phone for most of your life, you may wonder why you need guidance on using the phone in organizations. Using the phone in business can be a frustrating experience if you are not knowledgeable. If you follow these steps, they will enhance your effectiveness as a communicator.

✓ **Using voice mail.** Most businesses have discovered that voice mail is an inexpensive and convenient way to handle messages when employees are unable to take calls. When you hear a recorded voice indicating that you can leave a message in a "mailbox," remember to state your name, your position, your organization's name, the date and time you called, a brief message, your telephone number, and when you can be reached. Some people receive hundreds of voice mail messages each week; try to be succinct so that your message will receive the attention it deserves.

✓ **When to call.** The best time to reach people is just before lunch and just before 5:00 P.M. Many people are in their offices at those times. Remember to be sensitive of time zones.

✓ **Telephone tag.** Leaving messages helps to reduce telephone tag or that annoying process of people calling back and forth without reaching the desired party. When you leave messages, indicate when and where you will be and make sure you are at that number when you say you will be there.

Telephones

Telephones are not what they used to be. Changing technology has created many new ways to use the telephone as a communication device. You are already familiar with mobile phones, call waiting, and caller ID. The new generation of phones sport display screens, hideaway keyboards, and personal digital assistants (PDAs). Dick Tracy's wristwatch phone is now a reality.

CHECKLIST

Tips for Effective Teleconferences

Teleconferences are most successful when you follow certain steps.

✓ **Before the teleconference**

- *Identify the purpose of the teleconference meeting.* Let people know why you think it is necessary to hold the teleconference.

- *Identify the person who will chair the teleconference.* The chair is responsible for preparing the agenda, leading the discussion, summarizing information, and preparing the minutes of the meeting.

- *Schedule the teleconference.* After you obtain desirable times from each participant, select a time that fits in with each person's schedule and confirm that time with the participants.

- *Send an agenda and resource materials to participants.* Your counterparts will be better prepared for the discussion if they are given materials to review ahead of time, ideally three to four days prior to the meeting.

✓ **During the teleconference**

- *Start on time.* Teleconferences are expensive, and participants' busy schedules are best accommodated with meetings that start on time.

- *Ask participants to identify themselves when they speak for the first time.* It is distracting to hear someone talk without knowing who the person is. Participants then spend time trying to figure out who is talking rather than listening to what that person is saying.

- *Encourage succinct remarks.* A teleconference is no place for speeches or diatribes. Ask participants to keep their remarks brief.

✓ **After the teleconference**

- *Prepare and distribute minutes of the teleconference.* The minutes should include a summary of the discussion, a description of any overall consensus, and a section entitled "actions agreed upon."

SOURCE: James S. O'Rourke, presentation delivered to the Executive Conference, Sisters of Saint Francis Health Services, Inc. (South Bend, Indiana, 1993).

Teleconferencing

When participants are unable to meet in one location, teleconferencing is a popular technique for conducting meetings. Teleconferencing uses telephones to link people who are in remote locations. By using speaker phones, several people in one location can speak and listen to their colleagues, who are doing the same thing at different sites. Teleconferencing is an attractive alternative to centralized meetings since both travel time and costs can be significantly reduced.

E-Mail

Electronic mail or e-mail has become a common form of personal and professional communication. E-mail is cheaper than a telephone call and faster than the postal service and, therefore, serves an important communication function when time and money are an issue. Essentially, e-mail is person-to-person communication using computers and phone lines.

One reason that e-mail systems are so popular is that you can send memos to several colleagues at once. In addition, when you use e-mail, a record is

CHECKLIST

E-mail Etiquette

You can improve your e-mail style by understanding some of the important factors regarding e-mail etiquette and politics.

✓ Don't *flame*. (A flame is an inflammatory remark that contains insensitive language or impetuous negative responses.)

✓ Respect e-mail confidentiality.

✓ Make your messages as brief as possible.

✓ Eliminate sexist language from your e-mail, including masculine pronouns and gender-specific titles.

✓ Be culturally aware for both U.S. and international e-mail.

✓ Avoid using all capital letters or all small letters.

✓ Know when not to use e-mail. If the message is very important, controversial, or confidential, consider sending a letter, using the telephone, or having a face-to-face meeting.

✓ Use the SUBJECT line precisely so that it gives the reader the exact intent of your message.

✓ Avoid sending copies of your message to people who do not want it.

SOURCE: James S. O'Rourke, presentation delivered to the Executive Conference, Sisters of Saint Francis Health Services, Inc. (South Bend, Indiana, 1993).

made of the time you send your communication and the time it is received. Thus, no one can falsely accuse you of failing to send information.

Internet

The Internet is the largest computer network in the world, with hundreds of millions of users. Often referred to as the "information superhighway," the Internet provides users with a vast array of options for accessing information, news, and data; it is the largest information resource in the world.

The World Wide Web, the "Web," is one of the most common interfaces to access the Internet. By using applications termed browsers to access pages full of text, sound, and graphics resources, Web users can navigate the Internet more easily and productively. Hyperlinks, or connections, on a Web page can lead you to other pages where related information is located. Each of these sites allows for the retrieval of text, sound bites, and even video clips. Every month, more and more business organizations are using the Web to advertise their merchandise and services.

SUMMARY

As we have seen, the greatest difference between communication in dyads or small groups and communication in organizations is the structure of organizations. Within organizations, individuals are part of groups or teams that are organized into hierarchies; this means that some individuals or groups have more status or influence than others, but they are all interdependent. Both individuals and groups can be reconfigured (as in a department shake-up), with the result that different individuals or groups then communicate with one another. Still, the organization persists intact. An organization has its own culture (organizational culture), which interacts with the general culture to provide a constant interchange between the outside world and the organization.

# GLOSSARY

antigroup roles   Behaviors that attempt to satisfy individual rather than group needs, which are often irrelevant to the task at hand and are clearly not aimed at maintaining the group as a team.

attribution   A generalization that uses personal characteristics to explain communication behavior.

audience   One or more people who are listening to what a person is saying and/or watching what that person is doing.

authoritarian leadership   Control by a leader without input from group members.

centrality   The degree to which a member of a group sends and receives messages from others in the group.

centralized network   A type of network in which a majority of the communication passes through a small number of participants.

clique or coalition   An exclusive group held together by common interests and activities.

code   The symbols, signals, or signs used to construct messages.

cognitive forces   The perception, interpretation, evaluation, storage, retrieval, and integration of information input to an individual. In a group, one of the factors that influences group decision making.

cognitive processes   Mental processes referring to what someone thinks, believes, or feels, specifically involving the beliefs individuals hold and the methods they use to make decisions. In a group, one of the factors that influences group decision making.

cohesion   A group's ability to work as an integrated unit.

communication   A process defined by six characteristics: (1) symbolic behavior; (2) the sharing of a code; (3) its tie to culture; (4) intentionality; (5) the presence of a medium; and (6) the fact that it is transactional.

communication apprehension   Fear or anxiety associated with real or anticipated communication with another person or persons.

conflict   A struggle between two or more interdependent parties who perceive incompatible goals, scarce rewards, and interference from the other party or parties in achieving their goals.

consultative leadership   Leadership that bases decisions on the opinions or ideas of group members.

critical thinking   A method of viewing the world from a reasoned and proactive perspective.

culture   The shared beliefs, values, and practices of a group of people.

decentralized network   A type of network in which many participants have a number of connections to others.

decode   To physically receive a message (or other type of stimulus) and interpret and assign meaning to it.

direction   In some definitions, providing this is a key function of leadership; according to this view, leaders are people who structure, guide, and facilitate a group's activities and interaction in ways that will lead to a desired outcome.

dyadic communication   Communication between two people.

effective leadership   Credible behavior by which an individual inspires and motivates group members to achieve desirable group outcomes through interaction.

encode   To mentally construct and physically produce a message.

equifinality   In a system, the characteristic that final goals may be reached in a variety of ways.

false assumption   A conclusion drawn from faulty reasoning.

formal channels   The communication paths established along the hierarchical lines of an organization.

goal   The ultimate purposes for which a decision is made.

group   A collection of three or more people, usually not more than twenty, who share sustained, purposeful communication with one another.

group communication   The process of exchanging messages among a collection of people (three or more, and usually not more than twenty) for the purpose of developing relationships and accomplishing goals.

group evaluation   An evaluation of how competently a group performs as a whole.

groupthink   The tendency of group members to accept information and ideas without critical analysis.

hierarchy   In a system, the classification of a group of people according to ability, status, function, or other criteria.

individual evaluation   An evaluation of how competently individuals perform as members of a group.

influence   In some definitions, a key attribute of leadership; these views of leadership highlight the notions that leaders have an impact on other group members and that people who can influence others become leaders.

informal channels   The unauthorized communication paths in an organization; the "grapevine."

intentionality   The level of consciousness or purposefulness of a communicator in the encoding of messages.

interdependence   In group relationships, how the behavior of each member affects and is affected by other members.

interpersonal communication   The process of two or three people exchanging messages in order to share meaning, create understanding, and develop relationships.

isolation   A position within a group in which the member receives and sends fewer messages than do other members.

laissez-faire leadership   A leadership style that involves little or no leadership per se.

leadership   The exercise of interpersonal influence toward the attainment of goals.

medium   A vehicle to transport or carry the symbols in communication.

mentor   An experienced organization member who serves as a role model for a less-experienced employee.

networking   Communicating with other people in order to benefit from the connection.

networks   Communication patterns used within groups. See also *centralized network; decentralized network.*

nominal group technique   A process in which individuals work alone (in a group context) to produce a basis for discussion that reflects all group members' viewpoints.

norms   Expectations held by group members concerning what behaviors and opinions are acceptable in the group.

openness   A system characteristic that refers to a system's ability to correct itself.

organizational communication   The exchange of messages between organizational members or among members of different organizations.

organizational culture   Members' relatively stable perceptions of their organization and its norms and behaviors.

overgeneralization   A logical trap in which one piece of data is assumed to represent all comparable data.

participative leadership   A leadership style that involves a leader working with other group members to achieve a desired goal.

protégé   A less-experienced employee who looks to an older, more experienced, and well-respected employee as a mentor.

psychological forces   The personal motives, goals, attitudes, and values of group members. In a group, one of the factors that influences group decision-making.

quality circles   A system adopted by many organizations in the 1970s and 1980s, in which groups of employees from the same work area met on a voluntary basis on company time to analyze and solve work-related problems.

receiver   The person, group, or organization that decodes a message or other type of stimulus.

role   In a group, the function a member performs.

role conflict   A problem that arises when competing expectations for a group member's behavior are incompatible.

self-managing team   A group of highly skilled workers within a larger organization who are completely responsible for producing high-quality finished work.

sender   The person, group, or organization that encodes a message or produces a stimulus.

sexual harassment   Unwelcome sexual advances or overtures and requests for sexual favors.

shared leadership   Leadership that may emerge from any interested and talented group member, depending on the context.

social forces   Communicative influences such as language use and persuasion, present whenever two or more people interact with each other. In a group, one of the factors that influences group decision making.

symbol   A sign (usually a word) used to describe a person, idea, or thing (a referent).

symbolic behavior   Behavior that uses a shared symbol system.

system   A unique whole consisting of members who have relationships with one another in a particular environment.

theory Z   A team management approach in which both the manager and the other members of the organizational group participate in management decision making.

time pressure   In a group, the effects of a shortage of time on the decision-making process.

transactional process   A process in which two or more people exchange speaker and listener roles, and in which the behavior of each person is dependent on and influenced by the behavior of the other.

values   The enduring beliefs that individuals and groups hold about certain issues and behaviors. In a group, one of the factors that influences group decision making.

wholeness   A system characteristic that refers to its unique configuration; a system remains "whole" despite individual or departmental changes.

# NOTES

CHAPTER 1

1. F. E. X. Dance and C. Larson, *Functions of Human Communication: A Theoretical Approach* (New York: Holt, Rinehart & Winston, 1976).
2. P. Ekman and W. B. Friesen, *Unmasking the Face* (Englewood Cliffs, NJ: Prentice-Hall, 1975).
3. B. Whorf, *Language, Thought, and Reality* (New York: John Wiley Sons, 1956).
4. E. T. Hall, *The Silent Language* (Greenwich, CT: Fawcett Publications, 1959); E. T. Hall, *The Hidden Dimension* (Garden City, NY: Doubleday, 1966).
5. R. Buck, "Emotional Education and Mass Media: A New View of the Global Village," in *Advancing Communication Science: Merging Mass and Interpersonal Processes*, eds. R. P. Hawkins, J. M. Wiemann, and S. Pingree (Beverly Hills, CA: Sage, 1988), 44–76; G. Cronkhite, "On the Focus, Scope, Coherence of the Study of Human Symbolic Activity," *Quarterly Journal of Speech* 3 (1986): 231–243; M. T. Motley, "On Whether One Can(Not) Communicate: An Examination via Traditional Communication Postulates," *Western Journal of Speech Communication* 56 (1990): 1–20.
6. E. Goffman, *Interaction Ritual: Essays on Face-to-Face Behavior* (Garden City, NY: Doubleday, 1967).
7. J. Gordon, "Work Teams: How Far Have They Come?" *Training* 29 (1992): 59–65.
8. R. Y. Hirokawa and D. Gouran, "Facilitation of Group Communication: A Critique of Prior Research and an Agenda for Future Research," *Management Communication Quarterly* 3 (1989): 71–92.
9. W. W. Wilmot, *Dyadic Communication,* 3rd ed. (New York: Random House, 1987).

CHAPTER 2

1. J. K. Brilhart and G. J. Galanes, *Effective Group Discussion*, 7th ed. (Dubuque, IA: Wm. C. Brown, 1992).
2. D. O'Hair, J. S. O'Rourke, and M. J. O'Hair, *Business Communication* (unpublished manuscript, 1997).
3. J. C. McCroskey, "Oral Communication Apprehension: A Summary of Recent Theory Research," *Human Communication Research* 4 (1977): 78–96.
4. J. C. McCroskey, *An Introduction to Rhetorical Communication,* 7th ed. (Englewood Cliffs, NJ: Prentice-Hall, 1997).
5. McCroskey, "Oral Communication Apprehension: A Summary of Recent Theory Research," 78–96.
6. J. C. McCroskey and V. P. Richmond, "Communication Apprehension and Small Group Communication," in *Small Group Communication: A Reader*, 5th ed., eds. R. S. Cathcart and L. A. Samovar (Dubuque, IA: Wm. C. Brown, 1988), 405–420.
7. L. B. Rosenfeld, "Self-Disclosure and Small Group Interaction," in *Small Group Communication: A Reader*, 5th ed., eds. R. S. Cathcart and L. A. Samovar (Dubuque, IA: Wm. C. Brown, 1988), 42–49.

8. M. E. Shaw, "Group Composition and Group Cohesiveness," in *Small Group Communication: A Reader*, 5th ed., eds. R. S. Cathcart and L. A. Samovar (Dubuque, IA: Wm. C. Brown, 1988), 288–305.

9. J. E. Baird Jr. and S. Weinbert, *Communication: The Essence of Group Synergy* (Dubuque, IA: Wm. C. Brown, 1977).

10. I. L. Janis, *Victims of Groupthink* (Boston: Houghton Mifflin, 1972).

11. J. A. Jaksa and M. S. Pritchard, *Communication Ethics: Methods of Analysis*, 2nd ed. (Belmont, CA: Wadsworth, 1994).

12. J. L. Hocker and W. Wilmot, *Interpersonal Conflict*, 2nd ed. (Dubuque, IA: Wm. C. Brown, 1985).

13. P. H. Andrews, "Group Conformity," in *Small Group Communication: A Reader*, 5th ed., eds. R. S. Cathcart and L. A. Samovar (Dubuque, IA: Wm. C. Brown, 1988), 225–235.

14. Brilhart and Galanes, *Effective Group Discussion*.

15. L. R. Hoffman and N. R. F. Maier, "Valence in the Adoption of Solutions by Problem-Solving Groups: Concept, Method, and Results," *Journal of Abnormal Social Psychology* 69 (1964): 264–271.

16. This section is based on many works, including K. D. Benne and P. Sheats, "Functional Roles in Group Members," *Journal of Social Issues* 4 (1948): 41–49; C. M. Anderson, B. L. Riddle, and M. M. Martin, "Socialization in Groups," in *The Handbook of Group Communication Theory and Research*, ed. L. R. Frey, M. S. Poole, and D. S. Gouran (Sherman Oaks, CA: Sage, 1999), 139–63; and A. J. Salazar, "An Analysis of the Development and Evolution of Roles in the Small Group, *Small Group Research* 27 (1996): 475–503.

17. T. L. Albrecht and B. Hall, "Relational and Content Differences between Elites and Outsiders in Innovation Networks," *Human Communication Research* 17 (1991): 535–561.

18. S. Kanekar and M. E. Rosenbaum, "Group Performance on a Multiple-Solution Task as a Function of Available Time," *Psychometric Science* 27 (1972): 331–332.

19. J. D. Orsburn et al., *Self-Directed Work Teams: The New American Challenge* (Homewood, IL: Business One Irwin, 1990).

20. B. Dumaine, "Who Needs a Boss?" *Fortune* 121, no. 10 (1990): 52–60.

21. Orsburn et al., *Self-Directed Work Teams: The New American Challenge*.

CHAPTER 3

1. J. K. Hemphill and A. E. Coons, "Development of the Leader Behavior Description Questionnaire," in *Leader Behavior: Its Description and Measurement*, eds. R. M. Stogdill and A. E. Coons (Columbus: Bureau of Business Research, Ohio State University, 1957), 7.

2. R. M. Stogdill, *Handbook of Leadership: A Survey of the Literature* (New York: Free Press, 1974), 411.

3. R. Tannenbaum, I. R. Weschler, and F. Massarik, *Leadership Organization* (New York: McGraw-Hill, 1961), 24.

4. T. O. Jacobs, *Leadership and Exchange in Formal Organizations* (Alexandria, VA: Human Resources Research Organization, 1970), 232.

5. B. M. Bass, *Bass and Stogdill's Handbook of Leadership* (New York: Free Press, 1990), 546.

6. R. Y. Hirokawa, D. S. Gouran, and A. E. Martz, "Understanding the Sources of Faulty Group Decision-Making: A Lesson from the Challenger Disaster," *Small Group Behavior* 19 (1988): 411–433.

7. Hirokawa, Gouran, and Martz, "Understanding the Sources of Faulty Group Decision-Making: A Lesson from the Challenger Disaster," 416.

8. M. Rokeach, *The Nature of Human Values* (New York: Free Press, 1973), 5.

9. W. A. Green and H. Lazarus, "Are You Meeting with Success?" *Executive Excellence* 7 (1990): 11–12.

10. S. R. Covey, *The Seven Habits of Highly Effective People* (New York: Simon and Schuster 1989), 213.

11. J. Dewey, *How We Think* (Lexington, MA: D.C. Heath, 1933).

12. R. Y. Hirokawa, "Communication and Group Decision-Making Efficacy," in *Small Group Communication: A Reader*, 6th ed., eds. R. S. Cathcart and L. A. Samovar (Dubuque, IA: Wm. C. Brown, 1992), 165–177.

13. A. C. Kowitz and T. J. Knutson, *Decision Making in Small Groups: The Search for Alternatives* (New York: Allyn and Bacon, 1980).

14. L. A. Samovar and S. W. King, *Communication and Discussion in Small Groups* (New York: Gorsuch Scarisbrick Publishers, 1981).

CHAPTER 4

1. S. P. Robbins, *Essentials of Organizational Behavior* (Englewood Cliffs, NJ: Prentice-Hall, 1984).

2. R. B. Adler, *Communicating at Work: Principles and Practices for Business and the Professions*, 3rd ed. (New York: Random House, 1989).

3. P. Frost et al., *Reframing Organizational Culture* (Newbury Park, CA: Sage, 1991).

4. E. M. Eisenberg and H. L. Goodall Jr., *Organizational Communication: Balancing Creativity and Constraint* (New York: St. Martin's Press, 1993).

5. P. Monge, "The Systems Perspective as a Theoretical Basis for the Study of Human Communication," *Communication Quarterly* 25 (1977): 19–29.

6. S. W. Littlejohn, *Theories of Human Communication*, 4th ed. (Belmont, CA: Wadsworth, 1992); A. D. Hall and R. E. Fagen, "Definition of System," in *Modern Systems Research for the Behavioral Scientist*, ed. W. Buckley (Chicago: Aldine, 1968).

7. D. McGregor, *The Human Side of Enterprise* (New York: McGraw-Hill, 1960).

8. W. G. Ouchi, *Theory Z* (Reading, MA: Addison-Wesley, 1981).

9. S. DeWine, *The Consultant's Craft* (New York: St. Martin's Press, 1994).

10. H. J. Leavitt, "Some Effects of Certain Communication Patterns on Group Performance," *Journal of Abnormal Social Psychology* 46 (1951): 38–50.

11. M. E. Shaw, "Some Effects of Unequal Distribution of Information upon Group Performance in Various Communication Nets," *Journal of Abnormal Social Psychology* 49 (1954): 547–553.

12. T. Albrecht, K. Irey, and A. Mundy, "Integration in Communication Networks as a Mediator of Stress: The Case of a Protective Services Agency," *Social Work* 27 (1982): 229–235.

13. T. L. Albrecht, "The Role of Communication in Perceptions of Organizational Climate," in *Communication Yearbook 3*, ed. D. Nimmo (New Brunswick, NJ: Transaction Books, 1979), 343–357.

14. A. Baber and L. Waymon, *Make Your Contacts Count: Networking Know-How for Cash, Clients, and Career Success* (New York: AMACOM for the American Management Association, 2001).

15. K. E. Kram, "Phases of the Mentor Relationship," *Academy of Management Journal* 12 (1983): 608–25.

16. D. O'Hair, J. S. O'Rourke, and M. J. O'Hair, *Business Communication* (unpublished manuscript, 1997).

17. H. Witteman, "The Interface between Sexual Harassment and Organizational Romance," in *Sexual Harassment: Communication Implications*, ed. G. Kreps (Cresskill, NJ: Hampton Press, 1993).

18. This section influenced by C. Berryman-Fink, "Preventing Sexual Harassment through Male-Female Communication Training," in *Sexual Harassment: Communication Implications*, ed. G. Kreps (Cresskill, NJ: Hampton Press, 1993).

19. J. Simons, "Pagers Send a Strong Message," *U. S. News and World Report*, November 27, 1995, 58–59.